MISSION TODAY
an introduction to mission studies

Graham Cheesman

QIF QUA IBOE FELLOWSHIP

Qua Iboe Fellowship
Room 317, Donegall Square West
Belfast BT1 6JE

Copyright © Qua Iboe Fellowship

First edition 1989

Printed in Great Britain by the Bath Press, Avon

To Menita
This book and my missionary service is made possible
by all that she is and all that she does

Contents

Introduction 9
A Note on Teaching Students from this Book 11

Fundamentals

1. Mission Work - Definitions 15
2. Our Lord's Command - The Great Commission 18
3. Motives - The Five Loves 23
4. The Director - The Holy Spirit 28

History - and the situation today

5. Paul - the Biblical Pattern 34
6. The Conquest of the Roman Empire for Christ 40
7. Christianity in Europe 45
8. Roman Catholic Missions to 1700 48
9. Protestant Mission Work to 1790 53
10. The Modern Missionary Movement 56
11. Missionary Work in the 20th Century 62
12. The Unfinished Task 67
13. Indigenous Missionary Societies 77

Some Aspects of Modern Evangelical Missiology

14.	Cultural Anthropology	82
15.	Church Growth	91
16.	Mission to Unreached Peoples	97
17.	Social Responsibility and Mission	103

The Missionary and The Churches

18.	The Missionary Call	112
19.	The Missionary - What sort of Person?	117
20.	Incarnation	123
21.	Missionary Preaching	127
22.	Church Planting	132
23.	The Missionary as Servant of the Church	140
24.	The Sending Church	145

Postscript 151

Appendices

1.	Resources for further Information and Study	153
2.	The Lausanne Conference and Covenant	157

Introduction

It is an amazing and thrilling fact that in the last two hundred years since William Carey went to India as a missionary more people have come to Christ and more churches have been founded than in all the previous one thousand eight hundred years. It is probably also true that in the last twenty years more books have been written on the subject of mission than in all the years since the Church has been founded. But although there are now plenty of specialised books on mission and many light popular works, there is very little that will stand between the two as a comprehensive text book for a basic course in mission studies. This book seeks to meet that need.

The material presented was born in a Third World context. It began as a course of lectures on mission studies taught at the Samuel Bill Theological College in South East Nigeria, just at the time when I was closely involved with the missionary efforts of churches and students in that country. It is still designed to serve the great awakening to the task of mission which is happening all over the third world today.

I was encouraged to prepare the material for publication so that it may be more widely used, not only in the third world, but also in the west. Hopefully, this book will provide an opportunity for students and many others who are involved or interested in mission to learn in a systematic way and begin to come to grips with the issues that need to be addressed in sending missionaries in the twentieth century.

The book is limited in a number of ways for lack of space. The major emphasis is on cross-cultural evangelism and church planting but this in no way denies the validity and usefulness of medical, educational and other missionary work. The discussion of modern issues in missiology is limited to some of the major debates within the Evangelical community to which I very firmly belong. I feel that these choices make for the most usefulness in the circumstances and anyone using the book as a teaching resource can supplement as necessary.

Above all, if the reader is stirred by the Spirit to engage himself in the great task of missions out of compassion for the world and out of love for the Lord, then I will consider that much has been achieved with the help of God.

This book is divided into four sections. In the first section we lay the foundations. In the second section we take a brief look at the history of missions and comment on mission theory as it develops. In the third section we glance at important areas of debate and study in Evangelical missiology today. In the fourth section we treat missionary work in a more practical way as it affects the missionary and the churches.

I would like to record my gratitude to Mrs. Doris Taggart in the office of the Qua Iboe Fellowship and to Mrs. Maureen King and Mrs. Isabel Porter in the office of the Belfast Bible College for their careful and faithful work. I am also grateful to the Rev. Bill Leach and the Rev. Bill Clark for all their encouragement which has made possible the publication of this book. I wish to offer a warm thank you to Mr Patrick Johnstone of WEC and Mr David Porter of BMMF for reading the typescript and offering valuable suggestions which I incorporated into the final draft. All errors that remain and all opinions expressed remain my responsibility rather than theirs. My special thanks goes to the 1986 missions class of S.B.T.C. who first heard the course taught and whose constructive comments and encouragements were a real help. May those of that class who are now serving in missionary work find this material a blessing under God.

Graham Cheesman
S.B.T.C. Nigeria
January 1988

A note on teaching students from this book

It is a great privilege to introduce students to this subject for the first time and the lecturer should be much in prayer that the Holy Spirit will use the lectures in the heads, hearts and lives of the students.

This book must be regarded as a summary which the student will take away and to which he will add. It is not a set of teaching notes so the lecturer must know much more than is in the book for every lecture. The selected bibliographies will guide him in his further study. Life and interest should be given to the "dry bones" of the chapters with stories and illustrations from your own experience or your reading of missionary history and biography.

The course is designed for a full semester's work. The chapters are of unequal length and some will take more than one class period. Assignments can be set, filmstrips and videos can be shown and practical work done to supplement the book. Wherever possible, class participation and discussion should be encouraged.

The bibliographies will soon become dated in such a vigorously growing subject and should be supplemented as necessary.

FUNDAMENTALS

Laying the Foundations

1.
Mission Work - Definitions

"God had an only Son and He made Him a missionary"
- David Livingstone

Missionary work today is not in crisis but it is suffering from a gross lack of definition.

In the western church, attitudes native to 19th century missionary practice still predominate as we move towards the 21st century in a quickly changing world. New waves of interest fight for the attention of the missionary supporter and society, such as the current interests in urban mission, social responsibility, and work in Muslim lands. The old roles of missionary teacher and missionary doctor or nurse which accounted for such a high percentage of the work force of societies in years gone by are increasingly being judged as not "proper" missionary work because the place of western institutions is under review.

In the Third World, churches are unclear whether they want to maintain the term "missionary" for those who come from overseas because of the historical content of the word and the attitudes it still represents. Some are preferring phrases such as "expatriate co-worker" or "partner". There is also an indigenous missionary movement in those lands which were once designated mission fields which has difficulty presenting itself to a Christian public amongst whom the term missionary conjurs up visions of a rich foreigner very much in charge in the past and still generally holding down an important job in an institution.

There is a great need for a simple and clear definition of mission work and it is best to see it as consisting of two principles:

A Missionary is Sent

Our word mission comes from the Latin MITTO which means to send. It is of the same usage as the Greek APOSTOLOS which means someone who is sent. Of course, we cannot equate modern missionaries with the twelve apostles of the New Testament but there were other people sent by God and the churches who were also given the name apostle such as Barnabas (Acts 14 v 14) Andronicus and Junias (Rom. 16 v 7). So the missionary is someone who has gone from his own people and church to another people. He has obeyed the first part of the great commission which is to "go". Nowadays we would say he has crossed a cultural barrier. So a church reaching out to its own town is doing local evangelism. A person from Brazil serving in Japan is a missionary.

There is an exception to this rule. When a person is sent to another area of his own people that is in special need, particularly if such an area has no church, then he is a missionary but we describe it as *home mission* work.

A Missionary is Sent to Minister the Love of Christ

He can be sent to those without Christ and, in this case, he will show the love of Christ by preaching the Gospel and planting churches. He can be sent to areas of great physical or social needs and, in this case, showing the love of Christ will also mean feeding the hungry, healing the sick, working in the community. He can be sent to churches that are weak and in need of building up and, in this case, showing the love of Christ for his Church will include teaching and nurturing the congregations.

Our Lord said "As the Father has sent me, so I am sending you" (John 20 v 21) and all these works were characteristics of our Lord's ministry. Primarily, he *preached* the good news of the kingdom and told his disciples that this was why he was sent. He also *healed* the sick and demon possessed out of compassion. He also *taught* the young church-to-be, the disciples he had gathered around him. It was in these three activities of love that the kingdom came.

Mission work - definitions

We can set out our conclusions in a diagram.

	PREACHING THE GOSPEL	TEACHING THE CHURCH	HELPING THE SICK & NEEDY
LOCALLY	local evangelist	preacher	the church caring for the community
IN ANOTHER PEOPLE	pioneer missionary	Bible teaching missionary	practical or medical missionary

A missionary is a person sent by God and the church to a people other than his own to minister the love of Christ - especially by the preaching of the gospel and the planting of churches.

Selected Bibliography

Peter Cotterell - *The Eleventh Commandment*
   IVP, Leicester, 1981, pp9-21

John Stott - *Christian Mission in the Modern World*
   Falcon Books (CPAS) London, 1977 (1975)

J.H. Bavinck - *An Introduction to the Science of Missions*
   (English Translation) Presbyterian and Reformed, Grand Rapids, 1960

David J. Bosch - *Witness to the World*
   John Knox Press, Atlanta, 1980

2.
Our Lord's Command - the Great Commission

"If God wills the evangelisation of the world, and you refuse to support mission then you are opposed to the will of God".
Oswald J.Smith.

Mission is Biblical. It is woven into Scripture as a whole and can quite properly be seen as initiated with the promise to Abraham in Genesis Chapter 12. It was debated in Israel and Judah in the theological struggle between Universalism and Particularism (the book of Jonah is connected with that debate). It culminates in the vision of Revelation chapter 5 - people of every tribe and language and people and nations gathered around the throne of God. We will concentrate our study on the greatest missionary passage of all - the Great Commission. However, I advise the student to look up the relevant expositions of other passages of Scripture in the following books.

J.H. Bavinck - *An Introduction to the Science of Missions*
   Presbyterian and Reformed, Phillipsburg, 1960, pp.11-24

J. Herbert Kane - *Christian Missions in Biblical Perspective*
   Baker, Grand Rapids, 1976, pp.17-33.

The work of missions is the Church walking in obedience to Christ. This means that his last great command will be central to our motives and also to our understanding of the task - these are our orders from the Lord. There are actually five versions of our Lord's commissioning of his disciples, that is he quite possibly did it five times in five different ways. They can be found in Matt. 28 vs 18-20, Mark 16 v 15, Luke 24 vs 46-49, John 20 v 21 and Acts 1 v 8. Of them all, Matt. 28 vs 18-20 is the most comprehensive so we will turn to that.

Our Lord's Command - the Great Commission

The passage begins by laying the theological foundation for missionary work. Then, in one imperative, "disciple the nations", it defines the task. In three participles it tells us how to do it - "going", "baptising", "teaching". Finally, a promise is attached for all who take part in this great work.

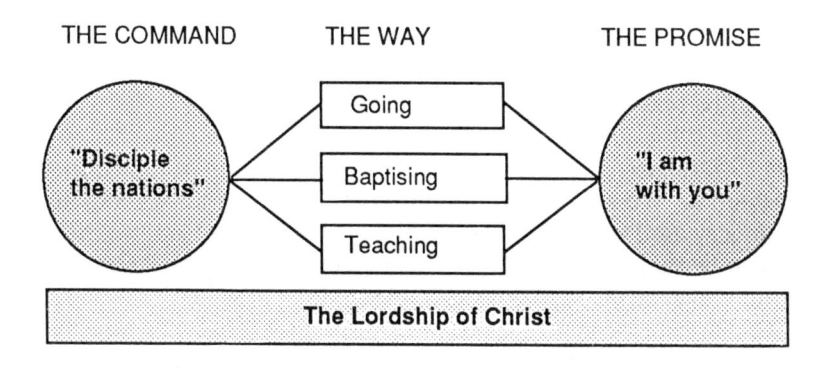

```
THE COMMAND        THE WAY              THE PROMISE

                   ┌──────────┐
                   │  Going   │
  ╱─────────╲      ├──────────┤      ╱─────────╲
  │"Disciple│◁─────│ Baptising│─────▷│  "I am  │
  │the nations"│   ├──────────┤      │with you"│
  ╲─────────╱      │ Teaching │      ╲─────────╱
                   └──────────┘

        ┌─────────────────────────────────────┐
        │      The Lordship of Christ          │
        └─────────────────────────────────────┘
```

The Theological Basis for the Task

"All authority in heaven and on earth has been given to me...... therefore ..."

The task of mission is based on the Lordship of Christ. The risen Lord has taken all authority over the world and the Church from the Father and so he sends out his disciples. Now the link between Christ's authority and the task is twofold:

1) His authority means he can command his Church. As the head of the Church (Eph 1 vs 21-23) he sends them out.

2) His Lordship also extends across the whole world. Every knee now has to bow to Christ (John 17 v 2, Rev. 15 vs 3 and 4). He now sends out his Church to demand the acknowledgement of that Lordship from every people. We go to proclaim Christ as *the Lord* and invite people to bow the knee now, for the time is coming when every knee will bow whether they like it or not. (Phil. 2 vs 10 & 11, Rev. 11 v 15).

We do not invite people to join our particular church grouping so much as to come under the Lordship of the Lord of the whole world and the whole Church.

The Statement of the Task
"Disciple all Nations".

In the Greek, this is the only imperative, which means it is *the* command. All the other words connected with it are participles and so describe how we are to obey this central command.

1) Disciple. A key word. It has all the meaning of the Gospel behind it. We are to make followers of Christ and throughout his ministry our Lord demanded the highest standards of commitment when he said, "follow me". "Unless a man take up his cross and follow me, he cannot be my disciple" (Matt. 16 v 24).
We aim at more than just believers, more than those who take the name of Christ. We need converts who come completely under the Lordship of Christ.

2) All Nations. Before, Christ was sent (and sent his disciples) to the lost sheep of the house of Israel;now he is declared to be more than the King of the Jews. He is Lord of heaven and earth. The opportunity of discipleship is accordingly given to the Gentiles as well. Every people on earth must yield disciples. God commands all men everywhere to repent. As we shall see, the early Church had to struggle to come to terms with this sweeping command.
We also struggle to see our responsibility to the whole world. The missionary task is the whole church reaching out to the whole world. Indians must not only be concerned with Indians, or even Asians but need to see their responsibility to the unreached in Africa, China and Arabia. Africans need a concern for Europeans, Irish for Americans.

The Fulfilling of the Task

The job is done in three stages:

1) Going. As we saw in the previous chapter, a missionary is one who goes. He or she crosses a cultural boundary, goes to another people to disciple. It is often the most difficult part of the task to say goodbye to your people and immerse yourself in a strange country. But if you stay at home you are not a missionary.

2) Baptising - into the Father, the Son and the Holy Spirit. This is the means whereby disciples are made. The Gospel is preached clearly and fully. Men are invited to repent and come to Christ taking Him as Saviour and Lord and sealing that in baptism.

In New Testament times baptism was often the occasion when a person reached out and took Christ. There is no reason why this practice should not be revived in mission work today.

3) Teaching. It was the practice of the early Church to teach the converts after baptism rather than hold any lengthy catechetical classes beforehand. The emphasis here is on the nurturing of the new believers, building them up by the Word of God.
Whereas baptism is a single transaction teaching is an endless process. The emphasis is still on the Lordship of Christ. It is his *commands* that are to be taught. It is to be comprehensive - *all* his commands. In Acts we see Paul preaching, baptising, gathering a church and then, wherever possible, staying a while to teach them.

The Promise With the Task -
"and surely I will be with you always, to the very end of the age".

If Christ sends a person, he does not go alone. Christ travels with his servants until the task is complete and the end comes. Notice two things:

1) It is conditional on obedience. "Go and I will be with you. If you don't go, don't expect my presence! I am going out to a lost world and, if you want to walk with me, come."If a church or group of churches today is without the evident presence and blessing of God it may be because it is not being obedient to the great commission and engaging in the missionary task. A missionary church is a live church; an inward-looking church is dying spiritually.

2) Christ enables the obedient. It is not easy to go. On top of all the natural problems of leaving your people and the opposition and hardship all true servants of God find in their work, it is a spiritual battle because the Lordship of Christ is extended at the expense of the kingdom of darkness. Christ with us gives the strength to overcome.

It is not a task we could ever do by ourselves. Men are dead in sin and we cannot awaken the dead by our preaching. Only Christ can do the job by the Holy Spirit he sends to convict the world of sin. Without him nothing would be accomplished.

This is the Great Commission. It is a trust put into the hands of the Church and of every church. Our task is to be faithful. How we can be faithful is the subject of the rest of this book.

Selected bibliography

J. Herbert Kane - *Christian Missions in Biblical Perspective*
    Baker, Grand Rapids, 1976, pp 45-50

David J. Hesslegrave - *Planting Churches Cross-Culturally*
    Baker, Grand Rapids, 1980, pp 22-26

A. H. McNeile - *The Gospel According to Matthew*
    Macmillan, London, 1915, pp 434-437

Robert Duncan Culver - *A Greater Commission*
    Moody Press, Chicago, 1984, pp 148-154

3.
Motives - the five loves

"Do you love me?" - Jesus. (John 21 v 17)

Why engage in mission work at all? Why go? Why pray? Why give? There is a theological answer to that question which touches the very centre of the Christian heart. As we look at it, may the Lord stir our hearts again by his truth.

It is a question of *felt* theology. Great doctrines which become real for us and produce the right kind of love in our hearts and the right kind of actions in our lives. This is especially true of the last two points.

Some of the motives below are false and wrong, others are partially good and partially bad. The last two are solidly biblical throughout. The contents of this chapter can be represented thus:

MOTIVES

1. FOR COUNTRY	2. FOR CHURCH	3. FOR SELF	4. FOR PEOPLE	5. FOR CHRIST
FALSE			TRUE	

Love of One's Country

One of the most frequent charges against missionaries is that they are agents of their country. In the earlier years of this century, they were accused of being agents of imperialism. Today, if they are Americans, they are accused of being agents of the C.I.A. Although the accusation almost never fits the facts, we have to admit that this love of country has at times overshadowed the authentic missionary task.

1) Imperialism is the attempt of one state to use another state for its own purposes. That happened in the 15th and 16th century Catholic missions. Occasionally Protestant missionaries partook of this in the heyday of the British Empire. Certainly many missionaries worked hand in hand with the colonial power, each helping the other. Nevertheless, the charge has been exaggerated. The attitude of most would have been that of Samuel Bill of the Qua Iboe Mission in Nigeria, who, after being presented with the MBE, came back from the ceremony amazed that people thought it all so important. Often, missionaries were hindered by the colonial power, and went beyond the borders of the colonial area, and they usually conducted an exclusively spiritual ministry.

2) Love of the culture of one's country however, is a motive which comes home far more powerfully. It was often part of the reason for missionaries coming out to Africa or India to bring to the people "Christian Culture" (By which they meant schools and hospitals mixed up with jackets and ties and the English language). Business and trade were also seen as part of the enterprise by people such as Livingstone and Carey. This was natural when a culture such as the western had so much to offer, but it was not properly thought out. The gospel judges all cultures and only those elements which are against the word of God need to be abandoned and only those which are clearly for the blessing of the people should be introduced. Unfortunately this was rarely done, and pride of culture was sometimes a motive for mission work.

Love of One's Church

The spread of one's own denomination has also been the motive of some, and part of the motive of many. A fierce loyalty to one's own ecclesiastical traditions has meant that missionaries have worked to plant more and more of their own churches in competition with others. There was a time of co-operation around the turn of the century where fields were divided up and the various denominations given different areas to work, but that has now almost universally broken down and competition is rife. It is an evil thing to the extent that it creates churches that have closer ties to churches of their denomination in U.K. or U.S.A. than to their own African or Asian brethren in the next village - or even in the same village!

This attitude has rubbed off onto the churches in the third world today and pride of denomination has hindered the work and caused much needless duplication. Mission work for the Presbyterian Church, for instance, is not to plant Presbyterian churches where there are none, but to plant Christ's Church where there are no genuine churches at all.

Love of One's Self

There is a wrong and a right sense in which this becomes a missionary motive.

1)   Self. Some people go to the mission field for purely selfish motives, and others for motives mixed with self. There is an employment crisis in most western nations, preachers in some churches find it difficult to get a job at home, others enjoy travel, some have used their position to trade. All such attempts to serve God and self at the same time are to be condemned.

2)   Spiritual Advantage. Yet there is advantage for oneself in missionary service. Paul says in 1 Cor. 9 v 23 'I do it all for the sake of the gospel that I may share in its blessings'. Mission work is good for a man's spiritual life. In difficulties and hardships, we are taught to rely on the Lord. Sharing the faith with others strengthens our own. Usefulness to the Lord is a great joy. It is an opportunity for real commitment. Stephen Neil has suggested that as monasticism provided an outlet for total commitment when martyrdom was no longer an option, so missionary work provided the same outlet for commitment for Protestant Christians when monasticism became no longer an option for them.

Love of the People

With this and the next point, we are dealing with theological imperatives - theology that should move and command.

1) Feeling for the people. The apostle Paul expresses this love for others in 1 Thess. 2 v 8, Acts 20 vs 17-21. It includes a love to the lost, based on the sure knowledge that without Christ they are lost for ever. Only a person who looks at the unconverted people to whom God has sent him and feels hurt often to the point of tears, can be effective among them.

Medical missionaries and missionaries working with relief schemes should have an equal love for the people in their poverty and sickness, and those who are serving the growing church should love them in all their need, feeling a brotherhood with them and suffering with them as a member of the one body, the worldwide Church. Jonah was a case of a missionary without love and pity, and God had to deal with him.

2) This love will show itself in urgency. It was present in the life of our Lord, "I must work while it is day, the night comes when no man can work". It was also there in Paul, "Do good while there is time". Opportunities will not remain for ever; the door of salvation will one day close. Other doors may close before that last great door closes. Open witness in some lands is getting more and more difficult. People are still dying without Christ in great numbers every day while we plan and postpone.

Love of the Lord

This is the supreme, and ultimately the only validating motive. If this is not there the work is philanthropy, but it is not mission. Before Christ commissioned Peter, he asked, "Do you love me?"

1) Love of the Lord will firstly show itself in obedience. The last command of Christ in the Great Commission needs to be obeyed and the Christian says, "I will obey because I love". (1 Cor. 9 v 16). A church not engaging in mission is a disobedient church, demonstrating by its disobedience either a terrible lack of knowledge of its duty or a lack of love to its Lord.

2) It will show itself in a desire for God's Glory. (2 Thess. 3 v 1, Phil 2 v 11). God's purpose is that every knee should bow, that the worship of our God should extend across the world so that eventually in heaven there will be those of every tribe and every nation around the throne praising God. God's people, all that the Father gave the Son, will be complete. The progress of the Gospel is the progress and display of God's Glory. Those who love to see God praised will feel this motive keenly.

3) Mission work is also connected with the love of Christ's final return in power. Christ's kingdom will not come until the full number of Gentiles has been gathered in (Rom. 11 vs 25, 26). There are an elect number for whose sake we need to endure all hardship so that they will come in and complete the Church (2 Tim. 2 v 10). All people must hear before the end comes (Matt. 24 v 14). God certainly works all things to his own timetable, but included in his plans is the obedience of his people, to do the job that has to be done before he will return.

All of us engaged in mission work of one kind or another, need to explore our hearts and sort out our motives in the light of God's word.

Selected Bibliography

J. Verkuyl - *Contemporary Missiology*
    Eerdmans, Grand Rapids, 1978, pp 163-175

David Bryant - *In the Gap*
    Regal Books, Ventura, 1979

J. Herbert Kane - *Christian Missions in Biblical Perspective*
    Baker, Grand Rapids, 1976, pp 139-196

4.
The Director - The Holy Spirit

"The coming of the Holy Spirit at Pentecost was the coming of a missionary Spirit". Roland Allen.

After our Lord gave the command to "go" to his disciples, he then said, "wait" (Luke 24 v 49). They could not move out until they had received the Holy Spirit. Looking back they would have remembered that our Lord waited about thirty years until the Holy Spirit descended on him at baptism before he began his ministry.

The work of the Holy Spirit is essential to the task of missions. Indeed missionary work is the work of the Spirit and it cannot even begin without him. This book concerns itself with knowledge and method, but unless it is all by and in the Spirit, nothing will be achieved for the Kingdom. We will look at his crucial role in three areas of the missionary task.

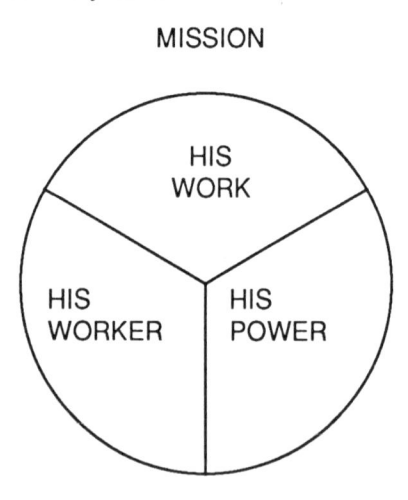

MISSION

HIS WORK

HIS WORKER

HIS POWER

His Worker - The Missionary

Our Lord told his disciples to pray to the Lord of the harvest to thrust out labourers (Matt. 9 v 38).

1)   They must be called by the Spirit. As the Holy Spirit said in Antioch, "set apart for me Barnabas and Saul for the work to which I have called them". (Acts 13 v 2), so it must be with every missionary. The Lord's great criticism of the false prophets of Jeremiah's day was that they went but were not sent. (Jer. 23 v 21, 28 v 15).

2)   They must be gifted by the Spirit. If they are to be evangelists, then they must have the God-given abilities of an evangelist. They then become God's gift to the Church. So it is with the other gifts of service that missionaries need. (Eph. 4 vs 11 & 12). Those the Spirit calls, he equips.

3)   They must be motivated by the Spirit. There is no harder task in God's Church than the missionary task. The missionary's heart has to be moved to go. All his dedication, self-sacrifice and zeal can only be maintained as he continues to feel the force of the motives we looked at in the last chapter. This is the job of the Spirit. Felt theology is only felt by the Spirit's work.

His Work - Strategy

The work is God's, not ours. The Holy Spirit accomplishes it all. He has his plans. He takes up men and women as missionaries and uses them as he wills. (Rom. 15 vs 17-19). This is a very important perspective for the missionary. It keeps him careful to walk close to God to discern his will, and gives him rest and peace when things seem to go wrong.

1)   The general plan was given by Christ. "Begin at Jerusalem, then on to Judea, then Samaria, then the whole world". (Acts 1 v 8). The book of Acts is a story of the Holy Spirit prompting the Church step by step along that road.

2) Special Guidance. The early missionaries were continually being told what to do and where to go by the Spirit. Paul in Acts 16 vs 6-10 was told to go to Macedonia; in Acts 18 vs 9-11 he was told to stay in Corinth; in Acts 22 v 18 he was told to leave Jerusalem. Philip was sent to the desert to meet the Ethiopian in Acts 8 v 26; Peter was sent to Cornelius in Acts 11 v 12. Livingstone wanted to go to China but was sent to Africa. Carey planned to go to the South Seas but was guided to India.

How can we hear his voice? Guidance is a large subject. What is needed on our part is:
    Openness. To expect to be guided and to be willing to go wherever sent.
    Closeness to the Lord. It is easier to hear a person's voice if you walk close to them.
    Experience. What is his voice and what is the sound of your own heart or the opinion of others? Experience makes it easier to tell.

His Power - Spiritual Life

There are impossible things to be done, but they are being done by the power of the Holy Spirit.

1) Moving a man's heart to Christ. This is not "just theology". This is how it really works! It is vital and real every time a person is saved. It is also important as an attitude on the missionary's part. Knowing this, we go humbly depending on God alone.

    All people without Christ are bound by Satan, lost in sin and spiritually dead. They need - and the Spirit alone gives - enlightenment (1 Cor. 2 vs 10-14), a tender conscience (John 16 v 8), the desire to be saved (1 John 4 v 19), the will to come (John 6 v 44), and new life from the dead (John 3 v 5, Eph. 2 vs 1-5). So, if a person repents, it is because God grants that person repentance (Acts 5 v 31, 11 v 18). No one comes to Christ without the work of the Spirit.

2) Church Growth by manifestation of Spiritual Power. Churches are founded and grow when the power of the Holy Spirit is seen to be at work. Miracles and healings led to many turning to

The Director - The Holy Spirit

the Lord in New Testament times (Acts 8 v 5). In the history of missions, great advances have come about through the demonstration that the power of the Spirit is supreme over satanic forces. It is our right to ask for signs to follow the preaching of the Word of God. In Africa and other areas of the world where the people see a clear link between spiritual power and sickness and accident and believe in land and territory belonging to evil forces, the spiritual power of the Holy Spirit needs to be seen to be working through the missionary.

From all that has been said in this chapter, two things follow:
 The missionary must be a person full of the Holy Spirit (Acts 11 v 24)
 Mission work is done by prayer for His power (Rom. 15 v 30).

Selected Bibliography

Roland Allen - *The Compulsion of the Spirit*
 (A Roland Allen reader Ed. Paton and Long)
 Eerdmans, Grand Rapids, 1983, pp 49-94

J. Herbert Kane, *Christian Missions in Biblical Perspective*
 Baker, Grand Rapids, 1976, pp 125-138

Michael Green - *I Believe in the Holy Spirit*
 Eerdmans, Grand Rapids, 1975

HISTORY
and the situation today

5.
Paul - the Biblical pattern

"Woe is me if I do not preach the Gospel"   Paul (1 Cor. 9 v 16).

In 10 or 12 years, from AD 47 to about AD 59, Paul established the church in four Roman provinces - Galatia, Macedonia, Achaia and Asia. Then, in Rom. 15 v 23, he says "Now that there is no more place for me to work in these regions, I go to Spain". He clearly counts his work there as completed.

Now this practice of Paul seems to fly in the face of missionary work as it has been done in the past, but we cannot dismiss it. The whole of scripture is written for our learning. The missionary career of Paul is recorded in such detail in the New Testament for our example.

Some have objected that Paul had certain advantages over us. He possessed great intellectual powers and a fullness of the Spirit, and was able to use the Roman empire with its ease of travel and protection. But he also lacked things we possess today - printing presses, radio, all of the New Testament, the ease and speed of modern travel. Every missionary situation is different, but we should begin to question our methods if our pattern of missionary activity is radically different from that of the Apostle.

Strategic centres

   1. Paul did not have an overall strategy, if by that we mean a detailed plan that he followed. In his first missionary journey, he was forced into Galatia by illness (Gal. 4 v 13). On his second, he tried this way and that until he was guided in another direction by

the Spirit (Acts 16 vs 6-9). He went out and the Spirit directed him.

2. However, he did follow a general method of working in a province. He identified the strategic centres and spent time in them, if necessary passing by other towns just as big, but which were not centres of trade, or travel, or of intellectual ferment. In other words, his ministry was deliberately urban and he chose centres from which the gospel would spread. When he could choose, he stayed longer at the most strategic places like Ephesus. Acts 19 v 10 sums up his strategy here, "All the Jews and Greeks who lived in the province of Asia heard the word of the Lord" - because of the ministry of Paul in that strategic centre of Ephesus.

Finance

1. The Apostle evolved a financial policy which he clearly believed contributed to his success as a missionary, partly because it determined his relationship to the people to whom he witnessed.

2. It was a policy which did not see money as too important for the spread of the gospel. We tend to believe that lack of money hampers all missionary effort. It was not the case with Paul because his methods did not depend on massive sums of money being injected from abroad. Peter and John at the gate Beautiful said "Silver and gold have I none", but they gave the poor man much more and went on to turn the world upside down without the use of silver or gold. Roland Allen summarises Paul's policy in three statements.

He did not seek financial help for himself. Particularly, he did not ask for support from those to whom he preached. There were plenty of religious charlatans preaching for money in Paul's day and he did not want to be confused with them. (1Thess. 2 vs 7, 8, 9; Acts 20 vs 33 & 34). Rather, he would work by night to be able to preach by day. He accepted gifts from other churches he had already founded and had left in order to work in a new area (Phil. 4 v 16, 2 Cor. 11 v 8).

He did not bring money to his converts. Each church he founded immediately became financially independent. The only exception to this rule was when he collected for one established church (Jerusalem) from other established churches (Corinth, etc) by way of an expression of brotherhood in special need. However, this was a collection from the new churches on the mission field to help the original sending church back home!

The churches administered their own funds. Even when he went to Jerusalem with the money from the provinces, Paul took with him representatives of those churches to carry the money. Paul kept his hands off.

Baptism and ordination

1. Paul's general practice was baptism as a confession of faith or soon after such a confession. The Philippian Jailor (Acts 16 v 33) was baptised maybe one or two hours after conversion. No doubt in each case Paul made careful examination to see as far as possible whether the person was ready, but no long delay is ever recorded. It seems that Paul only baptised the first few converts and then left the church to do its own baptisms (1 Cor. 1 vs 14-17). Teaching came after baptism.

2. Concerning ordination of elders, he appointed more than one in every church after a short while, sometimes about six months after they were converted. Often they would then carry on the task of appointing other elders themselves since we never hear of Paul appointing elders a second time in any church although Timothy did this for a while in Ephesus. The elders administered the sacraments, since they were the only ones available in a local church situation where Baptism and the Lord's Supper were regularly practised. In this way, a local church became self-sufficient and truly indigenous.

Teaching and leaving

1. Paul taught his converts systematically and carefully. They were to be the founding members of the church. But after teaching, he handed over the church to them and left. He founded churches, not missions. He taught them and left them, trusting the Holy Spirit. The usual period of time was about six months, but in

the case of some very strategic areas, such as Ephesus, it was three years. After that, he visited them and wrote them letters and, when they were in difficulties, sent them men such as Timothy or Titus for a while. Roland Allen says, "The shortness of his stay may have conduced in no small measure to St Paul's success".

2. The teaching seems to have been on doctrine and morality, with orders of service for the sacraments (1 Cor. 11 v 23) but not for the services of worship as a whole. In much, they were left to develop their own patterns which Paul later modified for the sake of edification and good order (1 Cor. 14 vs 26-36).

He founded missionary churches

The church from which Paul went out was a missionary church, since they sent him out in the first place. But possibly it was missionary minded because he had been the preacher there for three years. He helped to create the missionary spirit and then became their missionary. At Thessalonica, he founded a church, then wrote to them about a year later and could say that the Word of God had sounded out from them across the whole province (1 Thess. 1 v 8). At Philippi, he preached and people were converted; he moved on and the church immediately sent money - missionary support - to Paul in his next missionary stop at Thessalonica. They then continued to send support when they were able (Phil. 4 vs 10-19).

All things to all men

On the central issues of the Gospel, Paul never compromised - even if an angel from heaven preached any other, he was willing to anathematise him! But in everything else, he was flexible (1 Cor. 9 vs 19-23). The purpose of his flexibility was in order not to offend, and so win people to Christ. Circumcision, when it was demanded as an essential part of the Gospel by those in Galatia, was resisted strongly and he refused to have Titus circumcised (Gal. 2 v 3). When it was not made an issue of the Gospel, then he was happy to have Timothy circumcised in order to give him happy access to the houses and hearts of the Jews (Acts 16 v 3). A similar principle is at work with his instructions concerning meat offered to idols and his participation in a vow ceremony in Jerusalem just before his arrest. He saw that a missionary must not bring his own prejudices, culture and way of life with him when he comes with the gospel, but must be willing to adapt so as not to hinder the work.

Notes on application

We must come to terms with this biblical pattern in two areas of our thought and practice.

1) Our assessment of the missionary strategy of early missionaries to the third world. We are right to criticise them for often staying in control of the church, its sacraments and finances, for too long. They also brought too much of their culture and too many of their prejudices, making them a required part of Christian life. Nevertheless, they came with the Gospel and founded true churches at great personal cost. Let our gratitude therefore be overwhelmingly greater than our criticism.

2) Our aims and strategies as third world missionaries. We should move away from the popular notion of what a "missionary" in the third world is. He is not a foreigner holding an important job in an institution and bringing much finance from abroad. He is a Christian called by God to leave his own people and go to labour and suffer among another people in order to give them the Gospel. In such a situation, Paul's methods should be adapted and used.

Selected Bibliography

Roland Allen *Missionary Methods: St Paul's or Ours?*
 Eerdmans, Grand Rapids, 1962

Dean S. Gilliland *Pauline Theology and Mission Practice*
 Baker, Grand Rapids, 1983

F.F. Bruce *Paul: Apostle of the Heart set Free*
 Eerdmans, Grand Rapids, 1977

Donald Senior & Carroll Stuhlmueller
The Biblical Foundations for Mission
    SCM, London, 1983, pp 161-190

6.
The Conquest of the Roman Empire for Christ

"The Kingdom of Heaven is like a mustard seed" Jesus (Mark 4 v 31)

With this chapter we commence a section on the history of Christian missions mostly after the New Testament events had taken place. It must be stressed that this is only a brief outline to help the reader find his way around the subject. It is strongly recommended that you read at least one of the three main textbooks and that you take a delight in reading missionary history and biography whenever you can. There are no selected bibliographies for the history of missions. The student is referred to the relevant sections of:

    K. S. Latourette *A History of the Expansion of Christianity*
        Paternoster, Exeter, 1971, (1937, 65, 70)

    Stephen Neill *A History of Christian Missions*
        Penguin, Harmondsworth, 1964

    J. Herbert Kane *A Concise History of the Christian World Mission*
        Baker, Grand Rapids, 1982 (1978)

There are at least four reasons for studying the history of missions:

    We are able to rejoice and thank God for what he has done.

    The mistakes and lessons of the past become available to us.

    We see ourselves - those engaged in the missionary task today

- as just the latest in a long line of faithful men and women who have borne the cross to those without Christ down through the ages.

The example of such people can sharpen our vision and fuel our desires for greater dedication to the extension of Christ's Kingdom.

The great achievement

Christ died around AD 30. At his ascension he left eleven close disciples, 120 who also gathered in the upper room and others - in total about 500 - who witnessed his resurrection. Within 300 years, the Church had conquered the Roman Empire. Roman soldiers had crucified Jesus; now Roman soldiers marched into battle under the sign of the cross.

After an initial hesitation, the Church's missionaries reached out to the Gentiles. Christian traders and travellers took the Gospel as they went and the ordinary Christian by the radiance of his life and the words of his lips made a great impact on those with whom he lived. By AD 60, there was a church in Rome and almost every other significant city in the eastern part of the empire.

Towards the end of the second century (AD 200) Tertullian could say, "We are only of yesterday, but already we fill the world" and "We have already penetrated all areas of imperial life - cities, islands, villages, towns, market places, even the camp, tribes, palace, senate, the law courts. There is nothing left for you but your temples". To be sure, Christians were still only a small proportion of the population, but they were growing fast.

The last and greatest persecution of the Church arose under Diocletian, beginning in AD 303, but the Church stood its ground and even grew. When Constantine the Emperor himself was converted and issued his famous decrees of toleration beginning in 313, there was a large and powerful Church spread across the empire.

The Church by AD 313

Antioch, the city from which Barnabas and Paul had set out, had a large growing church that eventually (100 years after our date) contained between 20 and 50 per cent of the population of that city of half a million souls.

Asia Minor, where Paul laboured for twelve years, had a strong church in every city reaching out to the countryside around, although there were still pockets of paganism in rural areas.

Rome, legendary for its steadfastness in persecution and faithfulness in times of heresy, was at first a Greek-speaking church and so was composed mostly of the lower classes (although some prominent members of the court had also been converted). By 250 AD, it had one bishop, 46 elders and 7 deacons probably serving 30,000 or more members.

Gaul (France) and Spain had received the Gospel and sent representations to the earliest church councils. **Britain** probably heard the Gospel first through converted Roman soldiers and Tertullian even claimed converts in the wild areas of Scotland where the Roman soldiers did not dare to go.

North Africa heard the Gospel early. In Alexandria, a great centre of learning, a famous theological school under Clement and then Origen was soon established. Across North Africa the towns, such as Carthage and Hippo, were strongly Christian while the countryside spoke another language and was little reached.

Beyond the Empire, missionaries had carried the Gospel to Ethiopia, Armenia, the Goths and India.

In all, at the time of the first edict of toleration, it has been estimated that there were 50 million Christians; one quarter of the entire population of the Eastern empire and one twentieth of the West. Most were the poor of this world but there were also many of the middle classes - traders etc., some from the intelligentsia such as Justin Martyr and some of noble birth who had also come under the Lordship of Christ.

Why the church grew

The Church grew because God had prepared the way, the Christians were, in general, powerful witnesses by life and word, and because the Holy Spirit was poured out in great measure.

1) The World Prepared. The first century A.D. was dominated by the Roman Empire. It was at peace, travel was easy and swift. Roman soldiers protected people travelling with the Gospel on more than one occasion. It was a time when the civilised world spoke one language - Greek - a good medium for theological ideas, so Paul did not have to spend long years in language study. The Jews had penetrated virtually every town so there were people waiting for the missionaries to tell them about the Messiah. Many Gentile 'God fearers' were converted. In the empire there was a serious spiritual vacuum. The old religion was no longer being taken seriously, new religions were moving in from the East. All this was the work of God.

2) A Living Faith. The early Christians possessed, in general, a living faith and a burning conviction that these things were true. This led them to dedication and self-sacrifice for Christ. The sign of martyrs going to their deaths singing, of old Polycarp choosing death with Christ rather than apostasy before thousands, made a great impression. Like Saul, many who stood and watched a martyrdom later became Christians themselves.

Christians were also attractive people. In a time when society was morally degenerate, uncaring and unloving, a group which lived in love with each other in all purity and showed love and charity to the needy was a powerful advertisement for the Gospel.

3) The Power of the Spirit. Many signs and wonders were done as a witness to the Gospel. The Spirit fell on the Church as in times of revival, and he did his work of convicting people of sin in many hearts. It was a day of great things. This is the central, greatest reason for the growth of the early Church.

Once Christianity became the popular religion of the emperor and the empire, nominal Christians flooded into the Church and spiritual decline soon appeared in many areas.

Lessons from this period worth discussing:

1.   The importance of the Gospel coming at the right time to a people prepared and receptive.

2.   What a few people totally dedicated to God can do.

3.   Mission work flourishes in times of revival, and subsequent to such times.

7.
Christianity in Europe

"Carefully provide everything we shall need on our journey, not forgetting to place in the chest in which my books are kept, a linen sheet in which my aged body may be wrapped."
Boniface setting out on his last missionary journey.

In A.D. 400, most of Europe was composed of a number of pagan tribes, each with their own chief and often at war with each other. As the Roman Empire fell apart, the centre of civilisation began to shift to Europe and with it, the spread of missionary work. It is a two-fold pattern:

1. Forceful conversion of whole tribes, resulting in nominal Christianity.
2. Faithful work of genuine missionaries who either went to non-Christian tribes or followed the soldiers and tried to make the name a reality.

Many lost their lives in both situations. In this chapter we can only glance at a few areas of mission work in Europe from the fourth century onwards.

Patrick and Ireland

Patrick was born about A.D. 389. When he was sixteen years old, Irish tribesmen attacked and took him from his English home so he became a slave and a shepherd in Ireland for six years. Eventually he escaped and went to France where he became a monk. Then he had a vision calling him to be a missionary to his previous captors. "I heard calling me the voices of those who dwelt beside the wood of Foclut which is nigh to the western sea, and this they cried, 'We beseech thee, holy youth, to come and walk again amongst us as before'". He returned to Ireland about A.D. 432 and remained there until his death in 461. When he landed, the land was completely pagan. When he died, the Church had spread throughout the country.

His method was largely to plant monasteries in strategic places from which the monks could go out and evangelise the area. This method became the key to the missionary efforts of the Celtic church across Scotland and Northern England in later years.

Boniface and Germany

Christianity entered Britain with the Romans, but with the collapse of the empire, very little was left. It entered again from the North through the Celtic monks from Ireland and Scotland and from the South by a mission from Rome sent by Gregory the Great. Boniface (680-754), whose real name was Wynfrith, was an English monk until the fortieth year of his life. His initial missionary work was in Belgium. The Pope then consecrated him Bishop for the German frontier, with the task of mission to the German tribes. One of his first acts was to cut down the great sacred oak tree of Thor in Geismar and use the wood to build a chapel! Victory in such an encounter between Christ and the powers of darkness was soon rewarded by a large turning to Christ.

He was a brilliant scholar, a clever administrator but above all, a burning evangelist. He founded many monasteries, and churches. Soon however, his administrative work became burdensome to him and in 753, when he was almost eighty years old, he laid it all aside and set out as a missionary to a pagan tribe in Holland. While waiting for some new converts to arrive for service, he and fifty of his companions were attacked and martyred.

Charlemagne and the Saxons

The Franks (who have given their name to France) were the most powerful European tribe of our period. Charlemagne was a particularly wise and powerful king of the Franks who himself became a Christian and was crowned Emperor of the Holy Roman Empire by the Pope on Christmas Day A.D.800. He then set out to make Europe Christian by force of arms. The other great group of tribes

Christianity in Europe 47

was the Saxons, mostly of Germany and Charlemagne set out to conquer them for his empire and for Christ. As he did, he wrote conversion to Christianity into the terms of peace. Any Saxon who refused baptism was put to death. Many atrocities were committed on both sides. Nevertheless, hand in hand with this disgraceful policy went faithful missionaries who often died in the pagan reactions. Patience, pains and prayer eventually bore considerable genuine fruit.

Constantine, Methodius and the Slavs

The Eastern church based in Constantinople had, by A.D. 800, a long history of suspicion and rivalry with the Western church based in Rome, particularly when missionaries from both churches were sent to a new area. However, it also had its famous missionaries. Notable among such are CONSTANTINE and METHODIUS, missionaries to the Slavs, a group of pagan tribes to the East of the Saxons and North of the Greek empire.

They were noblemen, well educated generally and theologically. Some of their most notable work was in the creation of the slavonic script, and translation of parts (tradition says all) of the Bible into the newly formed language. They preached only in Slav and translated the liturgy. There was little fruit for their labours in their life and they struggled constantly against the opposition of western church officials. But later Christianity spread from their work through Bulgaria to Russia and eventually was founded the great Russian Orthodox Church.

Lessons from the period worth discussing:

1. The importance of demonstrations of the power of Christ over idolatry among pagan peoples (see Boniface in Geismar).

2. That the modern practice of sending young and inexperienced men and women as missionaries has no base in history. In earlier years only the best mature men were sent.

3. The importance of language learning and translation for abiding missionary work.

8.
Reaching beyond Europe - Roman Catholic Missions to 1700

"Missionaries will convert the world by preaching but also through the shedding of tears and blood and with great labour and through a bitter death". Ramon Lull.

As Europe gradually became officially Christian in the Middle Ages, true Evangelical Christianity declined. The Gospel of free grace by faith alone was obscured by a church which had become important politically and which stressed sacraments and good works in a wrong way. The bulk of missionary work was done by the religious orders such as the FRANCISCANS, the DOMINICANS and the JESUITS. Their vows of celibacy and obedience and their often intense dedication made them mobile and productive missionaries.

The two great maritime nations of the later Middle Ages were Spain and Portugal. To avoid competition between them, in 1493, Pope Alexander VI drew a line from North to South across the world just West of the Azores. All to the West of the line belonged to Spain; all new lands to the East belonged to Portugal. (The line was moved West in 1494 to allow Portugal to possess Brazil). They were charged with conquering the lands in the name of their respective kings and converting the inhabitants to Christianity. Missionaries operated in this period and there is much for us to learn from them.

To the Muslims

Mohammed moved from Mecca to Medina in 622 A.D. and so began the Islamic faith with the creed, 'There is no God but Allah and Mohammed is his prophet'. He united the Arabs and they soon conquered, on behalf of Allah, Egypt, North Africa, Palestine, Asia

Minor and most of Spain. France was attacked, Constantinople fell in 1453. They were the final blow to the widespread nominalism which had overtaken the church as a result of the "Christianisation" of the empire.

Missionary work to the Muslims in the Middle Ages was almost nil. The crusades had a religious motive, but the motive was not the conversion of the Turk. However, two figures stand out.

1)   Francis of Assisi - born 1181/2. This godly man made two unsuccessful attempts to reach the Muslims for Christ. At his third attempt, he accompanied the soldiers of the 5th crusade and made his way across the lines to the Sultan of Egypt. Received with great courtesy, he was allowed to preach to the Sultan. Francis then proposed a trial. He and the Muslim religious teachers should walk through the fire to see who worships the true God. They declined and the Sultan was not converted.

2)   Ramon Lull - born 1235. He was the first to develop a theory of missions to the Muslim world. Up to age thirty, he was a young, carefree courtier, but in a three times repeated vision, was called to Christ and Christian service. For the next fifty years, he showed himself a sacrificial missionary, a missionary statesman and a godly man.

He believed that there were three things necessary for the conversion of the Muslim: an accurate knowledge of the language, a book in which the truths of Christianity are clearly demonstrated by reason, and a willingness to go and preach the Gospel even if one dies in the attempt. He worked hard for the first two requirements, and in fulfilment of the third, went himself to North Africa four times. On the last occasion, he was beaten so severely that he died soon afterwards.

To the Far East

1)   Francis Xavier - born 1506. The founder of the Jesuits. He moved with the Portuguese eastwards, first to India in 1542 where he worked among a group of nominal Christians seeking to make their profession a reality. In 1548, Xavier met a Japanese in Goa and, fired by the news of that sophisticated but pagan culture and, in his own words, "Burning for the greater glory of God", he desired to preach the Gospel there.

He landed with two others in 1549 and stayed for two and a half years. Despite great difficulties, he succeeded in leaving behind three groups of converts. Other missionaries followed and once local chiefs began to be converted, the church grew swiftly. By 1600, there were 300,000 believers. Following the anti-Christian edicts of 1606 and 1614, a great persecution fell on the church in which about 2000 died including 62 foreign missionaries.

2) *Matthew Ricci - born 1552.* He reached Peking, the capital of China, in 1600. Using his skills as a clock maker and repairer and a map-drawer, he made himself indispensable to the Emperor. He aimed at the conversion of the higher nobility first. Ricci decided that if Christianity is to be acceptable to the xenophobic Chinese then it must look as little like a foreign religion as possible. He dressed and acted as a Confucian scholar, used a Confucian name for God and allowed rites in honour of Confucius and the ancestors to be practised by Christians on the grounds that they were civil, not religious rites.

By his death, there were about 2000 members of the church in China, some from noble families. Because of Ricci's efforts, other Jesuit missionaries were allowed to travel widely in China and by 1650, 250,000 converts were claimed.

3) *Robert de Nobili - born 1577.* De Nobili was the most famous of Catholic missionaries to India. An Italian Jesuit, he arrived in Madurai, the centre of the Tamil culture, in 1606. Missionaries had been at work there for some years but few converts had resulted. He saw the problem as cultural insensitivity - the Indians despised the Europeans for eating meat, drinking wine and other practices obnoxious to them. De Nobili adopted the Indian way of life, studied the Hindu scriptures, cut himself off from the little western-style church in the area and disputed with all comers for forty years. Many thousands of converts were made. They were not allowed to leave anything of their old way of life except their sins and all idolatrous practice.

To the Americas

In 1492, Christopher Columbus sailed west from Spain, hoping to reach India by travelling around the world. Instead he discovered America and opened a vast new mission-field. On his second voyage, he carried missionaries. What happened soon after was a great tragedy. Spanish and Portuguese soldiers (the Conquistadors) were sent to conquer the new land in the names of the Kings of Spain and Portugal - and Christianize the nations by force. This was not difficult with the modern weapons of the Europeans. Very soon the priests who travelled with the soldiers were baptising 10,000 a day. Those nominally made Christians were then subjected to a cruelty amounting to slavery. So serious was this in the West Indies that the native population died out completely and had to be replaced with slaves from Africa!

There was heroic resistance to this policy by some missionaries, notably Bartholomew de Las Casas who made seven trips to Spain to plead the cause of the native inhabitants. Others such as Peter Claver laboured among the African slaves brought over in terrible conditions. Most effective was the policy of forming settlements or "reductions". The Jesuits were prominent in this work, which consisted of the creation of protected villages where the inhabitants received Christian instruction, lived out their lives in relation to the church, prayer and Christian festivals and did useful work. Within the walls, no soldier had jurisdiction.

To Africa

According to the agreement of 1493, Portugal was responsible for Africa. Generally, the Portuguese were content to trade rather than conquer in Africa, but they founded missions in Congo (Zaire), Angola, Mozambique, Rhodesia and Madagascar.

The work in the Congo was the most successful. The first Christians were actually captives carried away to Europe. In 1491, five missionaries arrived. The King was converted, but proved unfaithful. His son seemed a more genuine convert and the fate of the missions rose and fell depending on the allegiance of the chief. An African bishop was appointed in 1518.

Other parts of Africa adopted Christianity for a time, often to gain the protection of the Portuguese soldiers against their enemies. Almost all Catholic work in Africa had died out by the middle of the eighteenth century. Present-day Catholicism in Africa came after and alongside the new Protestant missions of the last century.

Lessons from this period worth discussing:

1. The need of a clear Gospel for lasting work to be done. The Gospel will dictate the method.

2. The use of a trade to enter a closed land (See Ricci in China).

3. Cultural Barriers (See Ricci in China and De Nobili in India).

4. What is needed to reach the Muslims (See Lull's three points).

9.
Protestant Mission work to 1790

"I have one passion, it is He and He alone". Zinzendorf.

For two hundred years after the Reformation very little was done in missions. This absence in the Protestant camp was so clear to all that Cardinal Bellarmine and others of the Catholic church used it as a point of controversy. To them, missionary outreach was one of the marks of a true church, which they possessed and the reformers did not! Some reformers in reply went so far as to deny this. "The great commission was given to the apostles, they offered the Gospel to the whole world and now there is nothing else to do". The *real* reasons are threefold:

1. For the early part of its life, the Protestant churches were fighting for their very existence and had little time to turn to other things.

2. They were divided among themselves. Much energy was taken up in controversies between Lutherans and Zwinglians, Anabaptists and the Reformed, and even Lutherans and Lutherans.

3. They were not in touch with the New World and other lands. Only the Catholic nations of Spain and Portugal had the ships and navigational skills until the English and Dutch entered the naval scene later.

Nevertheless, these reasons are not enough, and we do well to confess with shame the lack in those early years of a missionary vision that should have come with a rediscovery of the Gospel. It was not a completely black picture, however, and we can give two illustrations. Both arose out of a revival of real personal Christianity in Germany called Pietism.

The Protestant Church of Denmark

At the end of the 17th Century, Denmark had an Indian Colony of Tranquebar in south east India. It could not find any Danish missionaries and so turned to the Pietists of Germany who sent Ziegenbalg and Plutschau. Plutschau lasted 5 years. Ziegenbalg was only 23 when he set out around 1706 and died 13 years later in India. He set out five principles of operation:

1. Church and school must go together so Christians can read the Bible.

2. The Bible must be in the indigenous language.

3. Preaching of the Gospel must be based on an accurate knowledge of the mind of the people.

4. The aim is definite personal conversion.

5. An Indian church with an indigenous ministry should be established as soon as possible.

In the 13 years of Ziegenbalg's ministry about 350 people were converted, his principles set the tone for much later missionary endeavour and his example was an inspiration to many who came later.

Zinzendorf and the Moravians

In 1722, a little band of persecuted believers migrated to Saxony in Germany and were given permission by Count Nicholas L. Zinzendorf to settle on his estate. Zinzendorf was an ardent Pietist and soon became leader of the groups. He organised them into a community known as Herrnhut - The Lord's Watch. Its characteristics were deep personal devotion and commitment to the Lord and prayer. Soon they caught a missionary vision and sent missionaries throughout the world.

The statistics are amazing. Within 20 years of commencing missionary work, they had started more missions than all Protestants had started in the previous 200 years. Very soon they had 3 missionaries for every member at home! Their zeal became famous. They went to the furthest and hardest places - Greenland, leper colonies, India, Africa and America. When one was asked if he was ready to go to Labrador, he replied, "Yes, tomorrow, if I am only given a pair of shoes". For the most part they were ordinary people; carpenters, farmers. Given their fare and nothing else, they went with a clear call to personal conversion and commitment - and their work lasted.

Lessons from this period worth discussing:

1. How can a church be orthodox yet not a missionary church?

2. The proportion of missionaries to communicant members is a sign of life or death in a church.

10.
The Modern Missionary Movement

"Attempt great things for God, expect great things from God".
William Carey

The "modern missionary movement" belongs in essence to the 19th century, although for such purposes, the 19th century should be regarded as beginning with the French Revolution in 1789 and ending with the First World War in 1914.

At the beginning of this period, Christianity was a European religion, although it had its outposts in many parts of the world. At the close of the period, the Gospel had been preached in almost every nation, all the main languages of the world had the New Testament, every religion had yielded converts and tens of thousands of missionaries were working across the world. Most church groupings in the third world area were products of this movement.

Origins

Two great factors triggered the movement - one secular, the other religious.

1. Colonialism - The Secular Factor . Up until the nineteenth century, Europe was comparatively weak and thinly populated. All that changed quickly with scientific inventions and the Industrial Revolution. The steam ship and train revolutionised communications and speed of travel. Mechanical power was applied to manufacturing and produced great riches.

Along with these means of colonialism, came the will to colonise. Until that time, the European was content to come and trade and then go, but in the nineteenth century, he generally came to rule.

The Modern Missionary Movement

Many European nations became involved in a struggle to colonise the rest of the world before the other. Holland, France and Germany all set up their flags in the third world. But it was the British Empire which became the greatest empire in history, occupying India, large parts of Africa, North America, Australia and New Zealand, many other territories, and virtually controlling China at one point. The English speaking world provided, and still provides, four fifths of all western Protestant missionaries.

As the Europeans spread over the world, with them travelled the missionaries. Just as the Roman Empire, in God's providence contributed so much to the early spread of the church, and Spanish and Portuguese Empires allowed great opportunities to missionaries, so the Lord used the colonial era to provide the means for the spread of the Gospel.

2. Revivals - The Spiritual Reason . At the same time as the Lord gave the opportunity to reach the unreached, he had also stirred up his Church to have the will to reach out. It was the combination of these two factors which led to the great missionary movement.

In Germany, the early Pietism led to Zinzendorf and the Moravians. They in turn influenced John Wesley. In England, God mightily used Wesley and Whitfield and the Evangelicals within the Church of England. In Geneva in Switzerland, and French Protestantism, revival occurred. Just as these manifestations of the Spirit were dying out, the second great Evangelical Awakening occurred in the United States of America and spread to the United Kingdom in 1858.

Characteristics

It was a movement of Societies. The missionaries, by and large , were not sent out by the existing machinery of historic churches, but by societies founded across or within denominations.

The first was the English Baptists, (BMS) in 1792, then came the London Missionary Society (LMS) which was founded with the aim of planting the Church of Christ across the world in freedom from all preconceived Western patterns, and drew missionaries from many denominations. LMS was founded in 1795. The Church Missionary Society (CMS) was founded by Anglicans in 1799 and the British and Foreign Bible Society (BFBS) in 1804. Soon other similar societies sprang up in America and the continent and began to send missionaries. As we shall see, these societies eventually developed a life of their own and soon became much more than sending organisations, usurping the role of the churches they founded. But at the beginning they were necessary tools of the Church to carry vision into effective action.

1. Bible Translation. This was a Protestant movement and so had a healthy emphasis on the Word of God. At the beginning of the century, there were translations of parts of the scriptures into about 70 languages. At the end, a hundred languages had the complete Bible, another 120 had the N.T. and 300 more had some part of the scriptures. The early translations were imperfect and often needed to be reworked, but a great achievement had been made.

2. Schools, hospitals and other institutions (such as printing presses, etc). This was an age of missionary work where the missionary generally came from a dominant culture with a lot to offer those to whom he went, especially in the realms of education, medicine and technology. So wherever missionaries went schools, hospitals, and other institutions were founded and ministered the love of Christ in a practical way, sometimes at the very highest level. It is unfortunate that soon many of these institutions grew so fast that they tied down the missionary to administration and diverted him from the central task of proclaiming the Gospel. In almost all countries today, these institutions are largely taken over by the government.

3. The Female Missionary. It was only in this century that the idea of single female missionaries was contemplated. But once it was permitted and seemed to work, a great flood of them entered mission work and by the end of the century, they outnumbered the men. This brought problems, especially in lands where the Muslim influence was strong, but their contribution, especially in the institutions was immense.

The modern missionary movement threw up so vast a variety of work that it is impossible to chronicle it in this book and the student is referred to the standard textbooks. However the beginnings, under William Carey, should be mentioned.

Beginnings

William Carey's work was a turning point in the history of missions and ushered in the Modern Movement. He was a Baptist pastor in a little village in England and also the village cobbler. God laid on his heart a vision for taking the Gospel to the world. He was inspired by the work of the Moravians, Jonathan Edwards and David Brainard. In his campaign to stir up his churches to obedience to the Great Commission, he did four things:

Wrote an Enquiry into the obligation of Christians to use Means for the Conversion of the Heathen, in 1792, against a hyper-Calvinistic inaction in his churches at the time. What the 95 theses were to the Reformation, this little book became to the Modern Missionary Movement.

Preached to a group of Baptist ministers in Nottingham in May 1792. His text was Isaiah 54 vs 2 and 3, 'Lengthen thy cords and strengthen thy stakes'. His main points were, 'Attempt great things for God' and 'Expect great things from God'.

Helped to found the Baptist Missionary Society in September 1792, the first missionary society.

Went to India in June 1793 as its first missionary.

In India, he experienced great difficulties from the life and climate, and also from the British authorities and soon travelled into the interior to escape this opposition. While there, he and his wife suffered greatly, but after five years, he had completed the N.T. in Bengali. Unfortunately, it proved to be unreadable and the work had to begin again! Encouragement came with the arrival of two colleagues, Marshman and Ward, and they set up in Serampore, a Dutch colony a little down the coast, free from British interference.

    Carey's vision of missionary work was a five pronged advance, each element being regarded as equally important and each pursued with equal energy together with the others.

Widespread preaching of the Gospel. This he did.

Distribution of the Bible in the vernacular. In 30 years, the trio produced 6 whole Bibles, 23 New Testaments and parts of the scriptures in 10 other languages!

Earliest establishment of a church. When all three moved to Serampore, they constituted themselves as a church and elected Ward the pastor, so any converts could be immediately brought into an established church.

Deep study of the religious background and thought of the people which Carey in particular set himself to do.

Training of an indigenous ministry as soon as possible. A college was founded in 1819.

Carey only began the modern work in that land, but by 1851, there were 399 ordained missionaries and their wives, 19 societies were at work and 91,000 converts in India.

Ending

The end of the era can be seen as the First Missionary Conference at Edinburgh in 1910. There were more than 1200 representatives from all over the world. The chairman was J.R. Mott (1865-1955) and his slogan, from the Student Christian Volunteer Movement was 'The Evangelisation of the World in this Generation'. The vision was very strong and clear and there was great enthusiasm that it could be done. However, factors in the early 20th Century cast a cloud over Missionary work and brought to an end the movement, in its optimistic, colonial form.

Two World Wars in 1914 and 1945 interfered with the missionary task and brought to an end the myth of Western superiority in morals and culture. They also led to the collapse of the British Empire and the rise of North America as the major missionary sending area. (North America presently sends two thirds of the western Protestant missionary force.)

The Russian Revolution in 1917 and the subsequent rise of communism as an alternative to Christianity across the Third World.

Nationalistic desires of the third world. These dismantled colonialism in less than a generation across Africa, Latin America and Asia and gave Christianity the flavour of the 'white man's religion'.

Liberal Theology entered and affected the mainline denominations in the West and soon dominated the missionary approach of many churches.

11.
Missionary Work in the 20th Century

"If we are to do what He commands, then we shall need to use every available me⌒ns". M. Goldsmith.

The 20th century has seen a number of important new tools for evangelism made available to the church through the growth of the communications industries in particular. Also, there has come a proliferation of specialist ministries to take account of the complexity and mobility of life in this century. Nothing will replace, or do such a good job as the missionary who goes and lives with the people, shares their life and shares Christ with them. But those tools and ministries mentioned below, if used wisely, are of great help in the overall task. Those feeling called to missionary work should examine all the options the Lord makes available for service today.

New tools

1. Christian Radio and T.V. This is a major means of evangelism in the world today. In 1980, there were 1,450 broadcasting stations and 13 main societies involved in the work, 960 million regular listeners and over 4 million letters received from them by the broadcasting stations. It is the only direct means of preaching the Gospel in the 45 or so countries of the world where the door has been closed to missionary work by Communist or Muslim governments. The major broadcasters have committed themselves to work together to make the Gospel available to every person on earth in a language they can understand by the year 2000. At present they only broadcast in 103 of the 271 major languages of the world. However, radios are not available to the poorest people. Hostile governments can 'jam' radio transmissions and good follow up is hard to arrange. Often this is done through postal correspondence courses.

2. Literature Work. There is a great hunger for any literature in many parts of the third world. With the advent of modern cheap printing and easy transport, literature is becoming a major tool of evangelism. More than half of those who claim to be born again say that literature played some part in their conversion. Not enough of the evangelistic literature is being produced in the country in which it is distributed, or by Christian nationals of that country, so it often lacks relevance and impact. It is ideal when the writing, publishing, printing and distribution are all locally based but this is seldom achieved. More third world missionaries should consider this vital ministry.

3. Correspondence Course Ministry. Modern postal systems now coming into operation in most countries of the world have created the opportunity for this ministry. An advertisement is made in a tract, other literature, newspapers, over the radio or person to person. People are invited to learn more about the Word of God through a correspondence course and the response is generally good. Today there are over 300 centres across the world preparing, sending and marking courses. It has been especially useful in connection with radio ministry, and many people have been converted or built up in the faith by this means - especially in countries where traditional missionary activity is difficult.

4. Missionary Aircraft and Ships. Remote tribes are reached and missionaries in such areas kept supplied and helped by missionary aircraft. Today there are about 476 missionary aircraft in operation in 48 countries. The Missionary Aviation Fellowship is the largest society working in over 22 countries. It is an expensive and specialised ministry, but of immense value for pioneer missionary work in particular.

There are three Missionary Ships in operation today; MV Doulos, MV Logos - both owned by Operation Mobilisation, and MV Anastasia - owned by Youth with a Mission. Each has between 400-600 crew and workers and they sail the world calling in at ports where they get involved in evangelism, literature distribution, teaching of Christians etc. One aim of this ministry is also to teach those young people involved in discipleship and evangelism.

New ministries

1. 'Tentmakers'. This is not really a new ministry. Paul made use of his secular skill a number of times (Acts 18 v 3). However, since the second world war, ease of transport and the crying need for skilled technicians and teachers in the third world continues to open many doors. Johnstone estimates that there are 60 countries in the world where this is the major means of entering to preach the Gospel and over 30 where this is the only way to get in. It is a difficult work. The hostile government may closely monitor the activities of all expatriates and the missionary is often lacking in fellowship.

2. Short Term Workers. Increasingly today, young people are giving between a few weeks to three years of their life to work in a missionary situation. Those with a short period of service do not have time to learn the language or enter adequately into the cultural and social situation so their impact is limited. But they can encourage local Christians, do literature evangelism or help in backup tasks such as building. Often they are greatly blessed themselves by working in this way for the Church. Many catch a missionary vision that either causes them to go on as long term missionaries or helps them to stir up their church when they return.

3. Student Ministries. There are about 20 million university students in the world and many more than that in non-university colleges. They become the most influential members of their society when they leave and take up employment. Many large organisations are at work in this area. Scripture Union, Campus Crusade for Christ, The Navigators and the International Fellowship of Evangelical Students (a fellowship of Christian unions in universities across the world). Many more workers, who have been students themselves and understand their needs and life, could usefully be employed in this ministry. Much useful work is also being done among those students coming from countries closed to the gospel to study in the West. If such students are converted they can become evangelists when they return home.

4. Bible Translators. One of the tasks of the pioneer missionary was to translate the scriptures into the language of the people. However, many of these early translations were of dubious worth. The 20th century has seen language specialists set aside for this work and trained to translate well. There are now Bibles in 286 languages and New Testaments in 594. This covers 97% of the world's population, but it is estimated that 723 languages still need translation work. Wycliffe Bible Translators is by far the biggest organisation . It has 4826 workers at present. Much help comes from the United Bible Societies. The job is a difficult one. It often involves first reducing the language to writing for the first time; learning it well; teaching the people to read and translating the Bible for them. Usually personal computers are used for the work. Such work in a new tribe, along with the preaching of the Gospel often leads to a strong church being formed.

5. Children's Workers. In the third world especially, there has been a dramatic increase in the percentage of children over adults. Almost half (45%) of the population of Africa is under 15 years of age! A large number of Christians were born again as children and this witnesses to the importance of missionary work amongst children. Some missionaries are engaged in preparation of Sunday School materials; others work with organisations that hold children's missions or operate in the schools and churches, such as Scripture Union, Boys' Brigade, Youth for Christ, Child Evangelism Fellowship, Fellowship of Christian Students and others. Care is needed not to pressurise children into unreal decisions for Christ but rather to lay the full ground work on which a simple, clear, mature decision can be made. It is a difficult specialist ministry that needs the best.

6. Urban Evangelists. Today, there are 309 cities each with over 1 million inhabitants and over 40% of the population of the world live in towns and cities rather than the rural areas. This percentage is growing fast. A modern city is a complicated institution with many ethnic and linguistic groups who all need to be reached with the Gospel. It is often difficult and uncomfortable work for a missionary in a third world city. But the opportunities are enormous because those who migrate to the cities, having pulled up their roots out of a rural situation, are usually receptive to the Gospel - at least for a time. Much theoretical work is being done on Urban Mission today.

7. *Relief Workers/Evangelists.* Medical and Social Work has always been a part of missionary labours, but this century has seen areas of the world go through immense sufferings as a result of wars, famine, earthquakes and other disasters. Some Christian aid organisations have been formed to minister the love of Christ in these situations. The best of them like World Vision and TEAR Fund minister to the spiritual needs of the victims as well by preaching the Gospel. This joining hands of Christian love and Christian truth has proved very effective for the growth of the Church.

Missionary work today is a large, multi-coloured picture and this should be reflected in our prayers and support.

Selected bibliography:

Patrick Johnstone, *Operation World*
    S.T.L./W.E.C. Bromley 1986 (4th Edition)

J. Verkuyl, *Contemporary Missiology*
    Eerdmans, Grand Rapids, 1978, pp 206-224

J. Cristy Wilson, Jr, *Today's Tentmakers*
    CRISTA, Seattle, 1979

Lausanne Committee for World Evangelisation, *Christian Witness to Large Cities*
    (The Thailand Report No.9) L.C.W.E., Wheaton, 1980

Timothy Monsma, *An Urban Strategy for Africa*
    William Carey Library, Pasadena, 1979

George Verwer, *Literature Evangelism*
    S.T.L. BROMLEY, N.D.

12.
The Unfinished Task

"As long as there are millions destitute of the Word of God and knowledge of Jesus Christ, it will be impossible for me to devote my time and energy to those who have both". J.L. Ewen.

In this chapter we want to examine the situation in the world in the light of what has been done already to reach every creature and estimate what still needs to be done. We will have to make use of statistics. It is legitimate to use statistics in the Lord's work - in fact the writer of Acts uses them on a number of occasions (Acts 2 v 41, 4 v 4) - provided the motive is right and we recognise their limitations. Statistics are only part of the whole truth about a situation. Part truth can develop into a 'half-truth' unless supplemented by first hand reports. We cannot use them for things it is impossible to count such as "How many people in the world are born again?" and we have to be careful to define things correctly since numbers will vary with definition (for instance when is a person 'reached' with the Gospel?) In any case, they cannot be accurate. The best we can say is "the facts are something like this".

The world today

The task our Lord gave to his Church to preach the Gospel to every creature is getting larger every day with the growth in world population.

> In the time of the Great Commission (A.D.1) 170 Million
> When William Carey sailed for India (A.D. 1793) 900 Million
> The year these lectures were written (A.D. 1987) 5,000 Million
> By the end of the century (A.D.2000) 6,200 Million

In other words, there are almost *thirty times more* people to reach today than had to be reached in the times of the apostles. Of course, although the task in this generation is thirty times larger, the apostles were only twelve men. Today, as we will see, there is a great Church and the number of Evangelicals in the world today is growing faster than the population explosion.

It is a different world in many other ways also. The world is divided into the rich nations of the North and West and the poor of the third world with, on average, the western person living at fifteen times the standard of living of the person from the third world. Great cities (over 300 with more than a million inhabitants) along with the many other smaller towns have almost half of the world's population.

There is a rich diversity of language and culture - 218 Nations, 5,500 languages and maybe about 12,000 different culturally distinct peoples! Yet the new communications industries that can fly us around the world in one day, allow us to talk to someone on the telephone in almost any country or to speak to tens of millions at once by radio or television have 'shrunk' this great world to a "global village" and begun a process of mixing up cultures and peoples - especially in the cities.

The vast majority of people in the world believe in God and worship either the one true God or a substitute of their own making. Man is incurably religious. Christianity is the largest and most world-wide religion but others are also strong and growing.

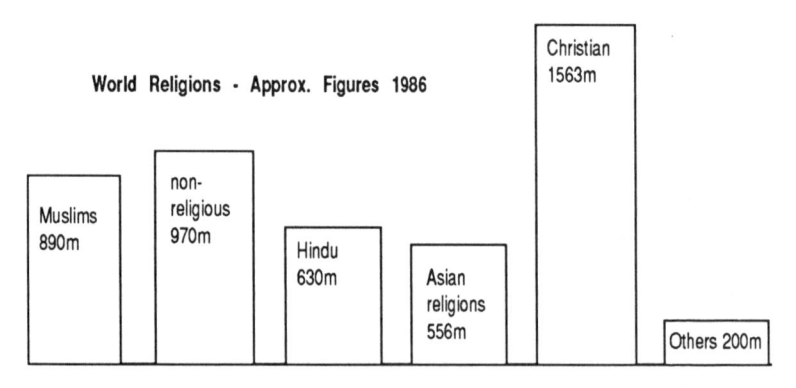

World Religions - Approx. Figures 1986

Religion	Population
Muslims	890m
non-religious	970m
Hindu	630m
Asian religions	556m
Christian	1563m
Others	200m

Others includes Jews 18m, Sikhs 17m, Traditional (Pagan) Religionists 100m.

THE MEANING OF

1. <u>People</u> Gen 17^7 ; Ex 6^7, 19^{5,6}

2. <u>Household</u> (Family) Gal 6^{10} ; Eph

3. <u>Temple</u> 1 Peter 2^{4f} ; Eph 2^{20f}

4. <u>Body</u> 1 Cor 12$^{12-14, 27}$; Eph 1^{22,23}

5. <u>Army</u> Matt 16^{18} ; Eph 6^{10f}

THE CHURCH (Ecclesia)

1 Peter 2⁹ᶠ → Called.
→ Covenant People.

19 → Born (Spiritually) into it.
→ God our Father (ABBA).

→ Where God is.
→ Where God is worshipped.

1-16 → Many parts, One Body.

→ Church Militant.

Non-Religious includes many atheists in Communist nations and the non-religious in post-Christian Western Europe.

Christian includes all those *calling* themselves Christians. Many are nominal only. About 926m. are Roman Catholic and 400m. Protestant. Of these, about 245m. could be called Evangelicals (that is those calling themselves Evangelical in non-evangelical denominations plus adherents to evangelical denominations).

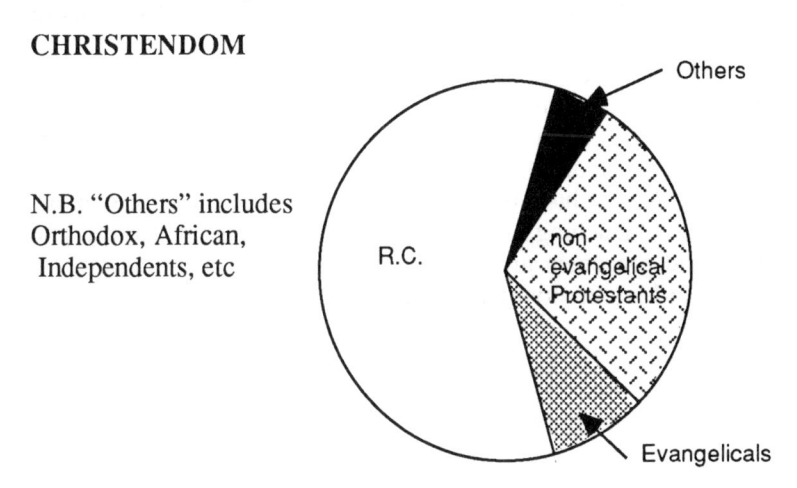

CHRISTENDOM

N.B. "Others" includes Orthodox, African, Independents, etc

Only God knows the hearts of men so no estimate will be given of those truly born again of the Spirit of God and so in the Church of Christ worldwide. Experience shows that even in the Evangelical Segment there is much Christianity that is in name only.

World Survey

The growth of the Church in the world has not been even, but has shown great variety. We now turn to areas of the world one by one.

1. Africa, South of the Sahara. (North Africa culturally belongs to the Middle East.)

There are, in black Africa, about 419 million people in 2900 different peoples groups, in about 15% of the world's land surface and 49 nations. The boundaries of the nations were drawn by the European colonists and so contain and cross tribal and ethnic boundaries. About 1730 different languages are spoken. Many economies today are in decline and there is much suffering of the poor.

20% of the people are still traditional worshippers, although this figure is decreasing quickly. 25% are Muslim and Islam is increasing dramatically as it moves southwards. About 54% claim to be Christian of which we have R.C.'s 15.8%, Independent Churches 5.9%, Protestant 17.8%, Evangelicals claiming about 11.4% of total population.

The growth of the church in Africa has been amazing. In 1900 there were less than 10 million. Today there are 225 million. adherents! But not all is good news. Much of this church growth has been nominal and many in the churches are still bound by idolatry. Others have been genuinely converted but lack even the most basic teaching. Good leadership is in short supply and untrained preachers are often in the majority. Persecution is a reality in Muslim dominated societies.

The task of church planting is by no means over. It has been estimated that 700 peoples groups are still without a viable church in their culture. As Islam moves southwards and Christianity northwards, the middle belt of pagan societies is a strategic area for evangelism. One great encouragement is that many churches are catching a missionary vision and beginning to reach out to other Africans in a systematic way. There may be as many as 2700 African missionaries today.

2. Latin America (South and Central America)
The population of this area is about 376 million., in 14.6% of the world's land surface. It is called Latin America because the countries of Spain and Portugal conquered it in the 17th century, settled the countries with Europeans and set up the Latin culture and language throughout.

Today 41% are Europeans, Indigenous 11%, Africans (who came as slaves) 7%, and those of mixed race (the results of intermarriage) 40%. The region has seen tremendous economic growth this century but the gap between the rich and the poor is very great. Historically the people have been Roman Catholic and in 1900 virtually the entire population was considered so. Since then Evangelicals have grown at an amazing pace - from 300,000 in 1900 to 34 million. in 1985! Today nearly 10% of the population

The Unfinished Task

is Evangelical Christian with three-quarters of that Pentecostal believers. Since many of the Catholics no longer attend church regularly, in most countries there are more Evangelicals in church than Catholics on an average Sunday.

The task falling to the Church is still great, but very different from that in Africa. The mixture of races and cultures has left few distinct "peoples groups" unreached. Great cities need more workers, so do students in the universities. Denominationalism and lack of unity hamper this work. Many have yet to come to terms with the poverty and social injustice and minister to that situation. Indigenous missionaries are being sent out by about 60 agencies but support for this in the churches is still small.

3. Asia (India, China, Japan and other lands of the South Pacific region)
Over half the population of the world lives in Asia (54.7%). China alone has 22% of the world's people - over 1,000 million. It is a large and diverse region, with almost 4,000 peoples groups and 1500 different languages. Communism has expanded into Asia since 1945, dominates a number of countries including China and is a potent force in many others. Nations such as Japan are rich, parts of India are terribly poor.

A large percentage (27%) of people grow up in Communist States with no exposure to religion and must be counted non-religious. In India the majority are Hindu (24% of total above). About 17% are Muslim and six nations, including the heavily populated Pakistan are Muslim States. Total Christians are about 7.3% or 193 million of which 2.8% or 71 million. are Evangelicals. In recent years some areas have seen dramatic growth. A hundred years ago there were no churches in Korea. Now in Seoul alone there are 6000 churches. In 1970 10% of South Korea called themselves Christians. By 1980 it was 20%! China is still closed to missionaries and it is hard to get reliable information out but a thrilling picture is emerging. When the missionaries were expelled in 1949/50 it was estimated that there were about 1 million Christians. Today there are between 30 and 50 million according to reliable estimates.

The Church is under great pressure of persecution in certain nations. In others, it is no longer alive as it once was. The Muslim lands still remain largely closed and where they are open, little results are seen. The Hindus of India, especially those of the higher castes and those who live in the north, are mostly unreached. China can only be penetrated by visitors or workers. A sign of real hope is that the missionary vision of the Church in Asia is strong and sophisticated. Asian missionaries can now be found all over the world.

4. Eastern Europe (Russia and the Communist block)
This area has about 400 million people, 8.6% of the world population. It is Communist in government with the power of the Soviet Union as a uniting force which helps (sometimes by armed intervention) to keep the nations faithful to Marxism. More openness is to be expected under the new Russian leader Mikhail Gorbachev.

Since the states are atheistic, atheism is taught in all schools. Churches are, wherever possible, hindered and controlled. Persecution exists for all who resist such control and many pastors and ordinary Christians have suffered in labour camps or prisons. However, the restrictions vary greatly from country to country. Albania forbids all churches. USSR and Rumania restrict and intimidate the leadership and secret churches exist. In Czechoslovakia, Hungary and East Germany, Christians are rarely imprisoned and there is more freedom. Poland and Yugoslavia permit most activities by Christians since the majority of the population are Catholic in Poland and Orthodox and Catholic in Yugoslavia. Some significant church growth has taken place - for instance among Baptists and Pentecostals in the USSR.

We should pray for God to open the hearts and minds of the leaders of these lands. Christian Radio is a useful tool of Evangelism, but the best means will be the Christians of those lands, despite difficulties and persecutions, reaching out to their own people. Some areas such as parts of Siberia and Central Asia Muslim lands are untouched with the Gospel and closed to mission work.

5. Middle East. (The Muslim States of North Africa, the Gulf and the Nations from Turkey to Afghanistan).
This is a large area of the earth, but most of it is uninhabitable because of lack of water. It holds 6.2% of the world's population, the majority of which are Arabs by race. It has, in general, become very rich in the last 30 years or so with the discoveries of oil and the

high prices paid for it on the international market.

Over 92% are Muslim and virtually all the lands are dominated by Islamic government and Islamic law. Christians are 4% of the total but this is very unevenly distributed, with 15 lands where there are less than 1000 indigenous believers. Seven of these have no indigenous church at all, and are completely closed to the Gospel. In some areas conversion to Christianity means death.

What can be done? This is the hardest mission field in the world - and doubly so today with the rise of a new confidence and missionary zeal in Islam itself. We can pray. We can send people as 'tent-makers', use Christian Radio and sometimes literature. There are a few Middle Eastern indigenous missionaries (estimated at 70) from Egypt, Jordan, Sudan and Syria who can travel more easily in this region than the Westerner.

6. The Western Nations. (North America and Western Europe).

This area includes about 13% of the world's population. Almost all are of European origin, and most speak either English, French or German. Three quarters of the population live in towns or cities. The standard of living is on average, 15 times as great as the Third World. Its political and economic power dominate the international scene.

The majority (75%) would call themselves Christian, although a growing proportion designate themselves atheists or not religious at all. 41% are Catholic, 29% Protestant and about 11% Evangelical. Church going in Europe especially is very low (about 11% in UK). The churches are often liberal in theology and ineffective. Even the Evangelical churches are full of materialism and are often inward looking and preoccupied with their problems. This is not universal, and there are presently 65,000 missionaries sent from the West. Some churches are alive and growing. Evangelicals in particular have grown in number and influence, especially in North America.

Much needs to be done in the Catholic areas of Southern Europe where many villages have no evangelical witness at all. Believers in the West need to come to terms with "post Christian society" and sort out ways of effective witness. In an area that has seen so much revival in the past, we need to pray for revival again.

The missionary task today

We have already seen that the missionary task is a wide one. It includes the showing of the love of Christ to all in need across the world. It includes the strengthening and teaching of those born again and formed into churches. It includes work among those vast numbers of nominal Christians such as Roman Catholics in Europe. However, what is plain from the statistics is that the greatest task is still to take the Gospel to people for the first time - evangelise the unreached.

Johnstone's analysis is particularly sensible. He sees two great Biblical goals:

1) To preach the Gospel to every creature (Mark 16 v 15)
Between 60 and 77% of the people of the world have had some exposure to the Gospel (although often this is very slight). So one to two thousand million have not heard.

2) To make disciples of all peoples (Matthew 28 vs 18-20)
There are to be representatives from every tribe and people around the throne (Rev. 7 vs 9 & 10). As we will see later, it is wise to divide people into ethnic and cultural groups into which churches need to be planted. There may be about 12,000 such 'peoples groups' in the world today of which 3 to 4000 have no viable church. These may represent one-third of the world's population.

Where do we find such unreached peoples? The majority are within the great religions of the world apart from Christianity - Islam and Hinduism especially; within the Chinese peoples of mainland Asia; and in unreached pagan tribes across the world. Winter gives the following statistics. 774 million Muslims, 561 million Hindus, 418 million Chinese, 264 million Buddhists and 135 million tribal peoples still unreached.

Some unreached people in proportion

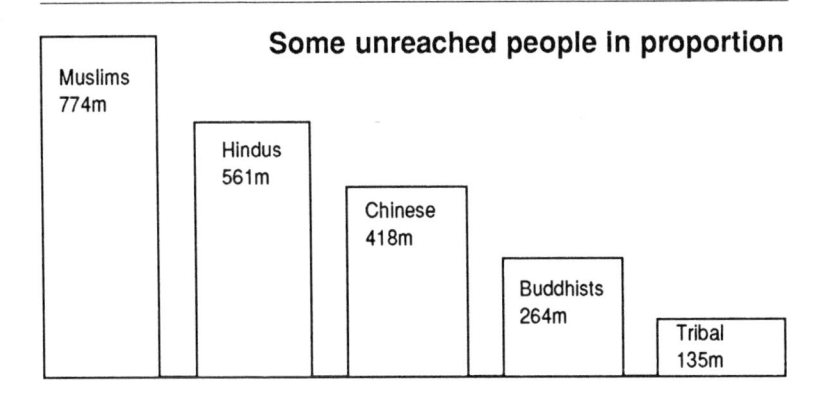

- Muslims 774m
- Hindus 561m
- Chinese 418m
- Buddhists 264m
- Tribal 135m

Deployment of the missionary force

There are about 81,000 Protestant missionaries at work today. 70,000 are from the West and Australia and New Zealand and 11,000 from the third world. The vast majority of Western missionaries are working with existing churches (93-95%) whereas the third world missionaries are more engaged than their white brethren in church planting (89), (these figures are very approximate). The numbers going are not at all adequate to meet the growing need of the world, or the immense complications of the task.

If this generation of Christians could all see their responsibility to the unreached, the worldwide church could certainly discharge its duty to evangelise this generation of lost men and women for the Glory of His Name.

Selected Bibliography:

David Barrett, *World Christian Encyclopedia*
    Oxford University Press, Oxford, 1982
    Updated in January of each year in I.B.M.R.)

Patrick Johnstone, *Operation World*
    S.T.L./W.E.C. Bromley, 1986 (4th Edition)

Ralph Winter and Bruce Graham, *Unreached Peoples*
    (Chart and Statistics)
    United States Centre for World Mission (USCWM), Pasadena, 1985

13.
Indigenous Missionary Societies

"The multiflow Biblical pattern of mission, mission to all the world and from all the world". P. Cotterell.

There is one great factor in the missionary scene which we have so far only mentioned in passing, but which may well prove to be the most important development in missions for two hundred years. It is the growth and maturity of third world missions.

After all, this is the Biblical pattern. A church is founded by missionary work, and soon begins to reach out itself. This occurred in Antioch (Acts 13 vs 1 & 2). It is a sign of the maturity of a church that it begins to do this and what we are seeing is the final stage of maturity of many of the churches founded during the great missionary movement beginning with Carey.

It is also sound Biblical sense. The great commission was spoken to all the Church; the task is very great and it will take the whole Church to reach the whole world.

The facts

There have always been third world missionaries. Very often they have not been remembered because the machinery of missions was geared to 'selling' the work of the white missionary in the West so that support could be raised. In Africa, many if not most of the big successful missionary enterprises have been by African Christians. Nevertheless, in the last 30 years there has been a great work of God in this area. We find two basic types of sending agencies, the mission board or society linked to a denomination and the independent society, a more recent development. These second types have a great flexibility and are often of radically different structure from the more traditional societies.

Today, according to a survey done in 1980, there are more than 368 sending agencies in the third world sending approximately 13,000 missionaries. Some have tried to link this finding with a previous survey done in 1973 and project the trend. They come up with the figure of 50,000 third world missionaries by the end of the century. What is more important is that these missionaries are returning to the first task of mission. According to the 1980 survey, 89% are engaged in church planting, (compare with between 5 and 7% for Western missionaries). We should not take such figures too seriously since they are certainly not accurate. Nevertheless, we are indisputably in the middle of an explosion of new mission work in the third world today.

Advantages

Such missionaries are theoretically more effective than their Western colleagues for the following reasons:

Less cultural distance. When an indigenous missionary goes to a new people in his own land or continent, he has less of a cultural and linguistic barrier to cross than his white counterpart so it is easier for him to do a better job.

Cheapness. It costs about £500 a month to keep a missionary from the U.K. on the mission field if he has a small family. This includes the very high air fares. For a Nigerian missionary, it can cost no more than M120 a month which, with the present rate of exchange, is less than £24.

Access. Often indigenous missionaries can go where others such as whites cannot. Muslim countries, members of the ECOWAS, are all more open to missionaries from West Africa than from U.K. They are not seen as agents of imperialism or the West. All this adds up to greater effectiveness.

A number of disadvantages are also coming to light and must be balanced against our initial enthusiasm. Cultural nearness sometimes causes problems of prejudice and rejection, there is a high casulty rate due partly to inadequate preparation and support and financial arrangments can often be difficult - especially when it requires sending funds out of a collapsing third world economy.

The situation in Nigeria - taken as an example

Denominations such as COCIN, ECWA, the BAPTISTS and CRC have founded their own societies or boards and have been at work for some years. EMS (the missionary society of the ECWA churches) was set up over 30 years ago and today has 600 missionaries, mostly in couples, all working in Africa but there are plans for work in South America, Greece and possibly Turkey.

Recently, however, the independent society has developed. CAPRO (Calvary Ministries) led now by Peter Ozodo has missionaries in unreached tribes of Nigeria, Gambia, Niger, and Senegal. It has recently moved into into Guinea Conakry with WEC. Christian Missionary Foundation led by Reuben Ezemadu has 21 missionaries scattered across Africa. Almost all of these missionaries are engaged in church planting in new areas. Often they are university graduates, committed young people.

In 1982 a number of evangelical mission agencies came together to found the Nigerian Evangelical Missions Association, NEMA. This organisation, the first of its kind in Africa, has already held two Missions Awareness Conferences, sponsors research and has a missionary training college in Nigeria for Nigerian missionaries. A similar tale can be told of many one time 'mission fields' across the world such as Brazil and Korea.

Partnership

It is time that the old western missionary societies realise that God is doing a new thing, and reorganise in order to get behind this new movement. Indigenous missions need support in prayer. For that the Christians in the West need up-to-date, well explained information but they are not yet getting this because our traditional societies are structured to project only their own work and workers.

They need support in other ways also. Some societies have

attempted partnership in personnel, such as WEC who are moving into Guinea Conakry in partnership with CAPRO, or O.M. who use indigens within their own organisation. There are difficulties with this approach, but it is one way forward from which both societies will learn a great deal.

They need support in finance. Many have, in the past, condemned the transfer of funds on the basis of keeping the indigenous church self supporting, not promoting dependence on the West and therefore slowing down that church's maturity. In the past this argument was very valid, but we are now out of such colonial days and the maturity and independence of such societies often exceeds those of the West. To continue to hold such attitudes is a form of paternalism. Western money can be accepted and used by third world missionary societies today provided it is done carefully. The example of the Indian Evangelical Mission is a wise one. They accept Western finance for missionaries outside India where the problem of foreign exchange is acute, and for special projects, but not for the regular support of their ordinary missionaries.

Selected bibliography:

Martin L. Nelson. *Readings in Third World Missions*
    William Carey Library, Pasadena, 1976 (with Bibliography)

Peter Larson, Edward Pentecost and James Wong.
    Missions from the Third World
    Church Growth Study Centre, Singapore, 1973

Lawrence Keys, *The Last Age of Missions*
    William Carey Library, Pasadena, 1983

THEORY
Some aspects of modern Evangelical Missiology

14.
Cultural Anthropology

"I become all things to all men in order that I might win some".
- Paul (1 Cor. 9 v 22).

We are all familiar with missionary tales of culture shock, and amusing (or tragic) clashes of culture. It is this area into which we move with this chapter.

We all live within a culture which we have learned (mostly unconsciously) from childhood and in which we feel at home. Ours will differ from every other culture in some ways and in many areas the difference will be profound.

Cultural Anthropology which deals with the understanding of cultures is a fascinating and intensely useful field of study which has greatly enriched missiology in the last thirty years. It is a wide ranging discipline that really demands a book in itself. Indeed, it is the integration of a number of disciplines; sociology, psychology, linguistics, phenomenology of religion, communications theory etc.

We can only give a brief outline of the main areas with which the cultural anthropologist involves himself and indicate some uses for the missionary. The bibliography at the end of the lecture is purposely more comprehensive than usual and can serve as an initial guide for rewarding further study.

Anthropologists and missionaries

Anthropology as a science (as opposed to the branch of theology bearing that name) grew out of the debate about slavery in the West. The issue was "How should we treat peoples of another way of life?" Some anthropologists stressed that we should study them, respect their cultures but not try to change them in any way. They were suspicious of missionaries who seemed to disregard all the good in another people's culture and engage in what came to be known as cultural imperialism - the replacement of, say, the African's culture with that of the West. Missionaries on the other hand felt that anthropologists were denying the people the right to make their own decisions and to change if they wanted to. They accused the anthropologists of relativism - that there are no absolutes, all cultures are as good as each other.

It is only in recent years that Christian missionaries in large numbers have come to see the value of anthropology and the truth in both sides of the debate. If you love a people, you will understand and appreciate their culture. On the other hand, if you love you will also allow them the right to change for the better where that is necessary and useful. From these realisations have come, in recent years, a large Evangelical literature making the findings of cultural anthropology available to the missionary.

Cultural anthropology

Cultural anthropology is the study of man in his social and belief systems and how they affect his life. It is a holistic view of humanity, the study of man as he partakes of the integrated system of learned patterns of behaviour, ideas and products characteristic of his society. What are the constituents of a culture?

1) Social Structure. Within each group of people there is social organisation. The Annang people of Nigeria are organised into families, villages and tribes. In England there are various social classes. In India there is a rigid caste system.

Kinship and relationship by marriage provides the backbone of social structure. Some societies trace descent through the wife (matrilineal), others through the husband (patrilineal). The marriage bond may be monogamous or, in the case of about half of the world's societies, polygamous - usually in the sense that one man has more than one wife, although a few cultures practice polyandry where one woman has several husbands.

In the West, the social unit is very much the nuclear family (one man, one woman and their own children). But many cultures see the most important social unit as the extended family most of whom will often have their home on the same compound. Most societies also form non-blood relationships such as secret societies. An example of these in England is the Freemasons; in Nigeria, the Ekpo society. Power and prestige are often sought through membership of such societies.

2) Roles and Life Cycles. Depending on the situation he is in at the time, the person he is relating to and his status in the community, each member of the society has a clear role to play. When a child addresses his father, when a wife lives with her mother in law, or when a man greets his neighbour, certain behaviour is expected of him and he learns that behaviour in order to meet the expectations of society.

Status, which affects the role and behaviour, is achieved by age, by the possession of riches, by birth or marriage or, by academic achievement. Societies will vary the relative importance of these factors. Today in Africa the status of the elder man and the behaviour expected towards him is rapidly eroding in favour of the status that comes from academic achievement, position in government or personal wealth.

As a person goes through the stages of life, his or her role and status change in society. The passage from one stage to another is often marked by a religious rite of passage. Birth, puberty and initiation into adulthood, marriage, old age, death, all change the role and status of the individual. A trivial example of this is the way in which a young woman in the church in South East Nigeria before marriage has to sing in the church choir, but after marriage, she is entitled to membership of the Women's Fellowship Choir and can wear a large head scarf!

3. World View and Religion This area of Culture has, of course, the greatest bearing on the missionary task and a concern to understand the religion of the people has always been a mark of the effective missionary.

All societies have sought to understand the nature of reality and have constructed a set of views of the world and God. They will include concepts of time, for instance, whether it is linear (tending towards an end) or cyclical (endlessly repeating itself).

Nature can be seen as divine or, as in the West, mechanical. Many societies do not divorce the natural from the spiritual and this is at the heart of the dispute in the churches in Africa today about healing. (The clash between the western mechanical model and the African model that assumes an interdependence between the natural and the spiritual.)

Ideas of God, his remoteness or interest in man, whether he is alone or shares spiritual reality with gods, spirits or dead ancestors, concepts of morality, all come in great variety in the religious philosophies of people.

Outward religion concerns the rituals and the specialists which put the person or society in touch with spiritual power or reality. Witches or sorcerers engage in black magic; diviners foretell the future; medicine men protect against witches, tell causes of sickness and heal; priests represent the people in rituals; and prophets speak on behalf of the spiritual powers. Individuals in certain cultures will often combine a number of these functions.

4) Language and Communication The current interest in cultural anthropology by those engaged in missions is, to a large extent, because of the need for accurate and meaningful translation of the scriptures. To say 'God' or 'Sacrifice' or even 'Shepherd' or 'Wife' in another language does not necessarily convey the same meaning those words have in English or, more importantly, in the original biblical language. The content of words is culturally determined. Communication is not only effected by language. Facial and hand movements are sometimes more important for the meaning than the words spoken. A man can shout "Ime!" and beckon, or shout "Ime!" and wave goodbye. The word is the same, the message is conveyed in the gesture. The expression of the face is even more meaningful and culturally determined. When Westerners are photographed they smile. Africans do not!

When a message has to be passed between two people, it goes through a complicated process. The idea is encoded in cultural symbols and language by the communicator and in terms of his own experience. What the receiver hears passes through his "cultural grid" and is also understood in terms he personally can understand with his own experiences of life. It can be represented thus:

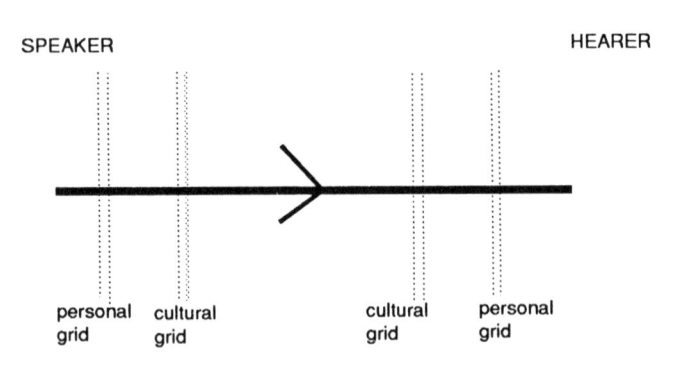

```
SPEAKER                                    HEARER

         |  |                          |  |
  ———————+——+——————————>———————————————+——+———————
         |  |                          |  |
     personal cultural              cultural personal
     grid     grid                   grid    grid
```

When two people of the same culture and similar life experiences speak, communication is easy and clear. But communication across cultures such as occurs in a missionary situation is a different matter which requires a lot of study and care if it is to preserve the meaning and relevance of the message.

5) Customs. These are ways in which members of a culture do simple everyday things. They are often related to deeper issues of culture but sometimes although their origins are lost in the mists of time, the practice remains very much alive. They can be styles and forms of production such as methods of working raffia, or art forms. There are many customs associated with food - the type of food eaten and the way it is given and taken. Certain foods must be eaten with the hands in Nigeria but this would cause offence in England. Tea must be drunk noisily in Morocco, silently in the U.K.

The most important customs are those directly related to personal relationships such as the way to greet a person; how to give and take things from another. Marks of hospitality and friendship, such as the offering of cola, the insisting a person partakes of a meal despite polite refusals are all "social lubrication" in society.

Usefulness for the missionary task

1) Recognising our Cultural Baggage. Missionaries have become notorious for not only bringing the Gospel to a people but mixing up with the Gospel the culture from which they usually come. The new convert then not only accepts Christ, but much of the missionary's life style as well - sometimes becoming not just a Christian but also a "little white man". This is unfortunate. The culture of the missionary works in his land because it has evolved there, and for that very reason it is unlikely to fit the receiving people. There is nothing more ridiculous than to see a man with a tight collar and heavy three piece suit in the tropics! You might just as well wear nothing but a light loin cloth in the snows of England! Unfortunately cultural baggage goes deeper than suits and ties and touches the way we think, learn, love and see the world. Cultural Anthropology helps us to distinguish between the Gospel, which we are commanded to go with into all the world; and our own culture, which we are not.

2) Avoidance of Offence Already in the section on the history of missions we have seen how cultural insensitivity blocks the growth of the Church. In Muslim areas of the world many things such as the drinking of alcohol, western dress, styles of worship, freedom and "immodesty" of women, eating pork, all turn the Muslim inquirer away from Christianity unnecessarily. In other places, offence can be given by wrong forms of greeting, the crossing of the legs or giving with the wrong hand. It is not up to the people who welcome you to make allowances for you. You must learn their ways and so avoid the giving of unintentional offence.

3) Understanding what goes on in Conversion Much study is being done within Cultural Anthropology today in connection with culture change. All cultures are changing, usually slowly because there are built in mechanisms to maintain the status quo. When the Gospel comes, however careful the missionary is to avoid unnecessary cultural upheaval, some significant cultural changes must go along with conversion. The Gospel judges every culture because every culture is constructed by sinful men. People can never think and act the same way as before if they are to be true disciples of Christ. As we have seen, the culture of a people is an integrated whole and changes in one area will cause repercussions in many others. So culture change brought about by conversion is particularly radical when idolatry is woven into most areas of social life.

It is often wisest to let the new believers make the necessary changes themselves as they see necessary (with the guidance of the missionary as to general principles). After all, they are the ones who know the cultural system best. It may also be wise to make valid substitutes for cultural elements that have to be dropped - simple harvest festivals in place of idolatrous new yam festivals, for instance, so as not to leave a cultural vacuum.

4) Establishing Indigenous Churches The New Testament lays down the theological basis for the Church and its life, and its basic structure. Each culture down through the ages and across the world has then, to a greater or lesser extent, enculturalised this by evolving those details of form and practice which are suitable for their culture. This accounts for much of the variety in the church across the world today.

For the missionary to import his church which was formed in his culture on to the mission field in its entirety is to guarantee a "bad fit". It will unnecessarily reinforce the impression that what the missionary brings is a foreign religion and will probably bring much trouble in the church in the second or third generation. Areas such as church buildings, detailed structure of authority and government in the church, church music, ecclesiastical dress, methods of teaching, can and should be indigenous to the culture unless the people themselves request otherwise for good reason.

Cross cultural communication

The missionary has to understand three cultures; the Biblical culture, so he can discern the meaning clearly; his own culture (which for the average third world missionary is a mixture of western and third world elements) so he can avoid an alien presentation; and the culture of the people to whom he ministers.

The last is the most vital, since, as we have seen, messages to a person pass through their cultural grid and are distorted before being received. The communicator needs to know how his message will be distorted. Can he use the people's word for God or does it mean someone very different from the God of the Bible? When he talks about Jesus as the high priest, how does their idea of a priest in their pagan religion "colour" the concept in a wrong way? Every concept or analogy (for that is what so much of theology is) has a positive and negative content. Jesus is a son in this way but not in that way. As a concept crosses a cultural barrier, the balance between positive and negative elements shifts, sometimes so radically that an analogy which is of great use in one culture has to be used carefully and sparingly in another. Shepherds in England are not like shepherds in Palestine. Shepherds in Nigeria are unlike shepherds in Palestine in different ways!

In communicating the Gospel, the missionary must work from a good understanding of the culture of the people, particularly the religious content of words such as sin, God, salvation, love, grace, faith, which are at the heart of the Gospel. He must move slowly and establish ways of getting thoughtful feed back from his audience. This way he can check, at each point, whether the meaning that is in his mind is being received and understood in the minds of the hearers.

Much more could be said about Cultural Anthropology and its uses for the missionary. In particular, the way in which it helps us communicate effectively the message of Christ should be studied further by all who seriously consider cross-cultural missionary work.

Selected bibliography

Eugene A. Nida, *Customs and Culture*
 William Carey Library, Pasadena, 1983 (1954)

Eugene A Nida, *Message and Mission*
 William Carey Library, Pasadena, 1975 (1960)

Paul G. Hiebert, *Cultural Anthropology*
 Baker, Grand Rapids, 1983 (1976)

Paul G. Hiebert, *Anthropological Insights for Missionaries*
 Baker, Grand Rapids, 1985

(Ed.) William A. Smalley, *Readings in Missionary Anthropology II*
 William Carey Library, Pasadena, 1978

David J. Hesselgrave, *Communicating Christ Cross-Culturally*
 Zordervan, Grand Rapids, 1978

Charles Kraft, *Christianity in Culture*
Orbis Books (Mary Knoll), New York 1979

Lyman E. Reed, *Preparing Missionaries for Inter Cultural Communication*
William Carey Library, Pasadena, 1985

David Smith, *The Communication of the Christian Faith in Africa*
Emem Publications, Aberdeen, 1983

(Ed) John R W Stott and Robert Coote, *Down to Earth : Studies in Christianity and Culture*
Eerdmans, Grand Rapids, 1980

Stephen A. Grunlan and Marvin K. Mayers, *Cultural Anthropology*
Zondervan, Grand Rapids, 1979

15.
Church Growth

"It is God's will that churches grow". Donald McGavran.

The founder of the Church Growth school of missiology is Donald McGavran who worked for some years as a missionary in India. His first book was *Christian Mission in India,* 1936 but the key text that launched the movement was *Bridges of God* in 1955. In *Understanding Church Growth,* 1970 he provided a more comprehensive textbook on the subject, which was revised and material added relating to church growth in the West in 1980. It represents a more mature and thoughtful approach than *Bridges of God.*

The Institute of Church Growth, now located in the school of World Missions in Fuller Theological Seminary, Pasadena, California, with, until recently, McGavran as Dean has been very influential in spreading the ideas and important for collecting research on the topic. Three other men are outstanding in this respect - all one time colleagues of McGavran at Fuller - Peter Wagner, Arthur Glasser and Ralph Winter. Eddie Gibbs is an English spokesman, now also at Fuller.

Church Growth is an influential school in Missiology today, despite criticism, and we have much to learn from it. Our method will be to state a proposition of the Church Growth School, explain it and then react to it.

The primacy of evangelism and church planting

Social work and nurturing of the congregation are both very important, but not so important as bringing in new converts and founding new churches. The churches today have lost this priority and we need to call them back to it.

Reaction: The call back to the primacy of evangelism is welcome and right.

However, teaching is also part of the Great Commission because Church Growth is an inward qualitative thing as well as an outward, quantitative thing. Both depend on the other.

Numerical growth must be charted, looked for, analysed and goals established

It is God's purpose that churches grow. We must use statistics to find out how and when churches grow, and to search out reasons for each up or down on the graph. We should expect that churches will grow and set goals to focus our prayer and activity.

Reaction: The emphasis on numerical growth has exposed an hypocrisy which we often have about numbers. We *can* quote numbers and should mourn when numbers do not come in. We should constantly assess our work in the light of its success or otherwise numerically.

However, it is a great weakness to stress numerical growth almost exclusively since that is a bad overall indication of real, spirit led, growth. Numerical growth can simply mean that many nominal Christians are adding themselves to the church such as occurred after the conversion of Constantine in the 4thC. Other indicators of church growth are the deepening of spiritual life, a greater understanding of the faith and joyful service.

"Men like to become Christians without crossing racial, linguistic and class barriers"

The world is a mosaic of ethnic units, overlapping, yet distinct. Evangelism by a church within its own ethnic, cultural group is the most effective.

Reaction: This must be acknowledged and acted upon. It is a good principle for general witness. Let a church be planted in all tribes and nations and let people be evangelised by their own people as far as possible. As McGavran says, "Most opposition to the Christian religion arises not from theological but social causes". This is true from a worldly point of view. Also, within a church, let the members be encouraged to reach out to their own groups, "beginning at Jerusalem".

But part of the offence of the cross is the *breaking* of cultural exclusiveness. We cannot leave this teaching until men and women are converted and gathered into churches since, in many circumstances, it must be preached as part of the cost. Converts must be invited into a church where there are no slaves or free, Jews or Greeks. See the next point.

Homogeneous unit churches are best for church growth

This principle must be applied sensibly, but for growth, a church is far better placed if it is made up of the type of people that they themselves are trying to reach. Each homogeneous unit (a people's group with a distinctive culture, language, class, or self-image) should have its own church for that type of people.

Reaction: This is at odds with the New Testament practice. It is also against N.T.Theology.

The new humanity in Christ is a body where different people find a common identity in one Lord. The unity and catholicity of the worldwide church must be reflected at the local level. It is unattractive if the church only reflects the existing social racial divisions in a society (see S. Africa). A concession to the weakness of men for the sake of numerical growth can never be permitted. It seems justified, however, when a group is only at home in one language. It cannot meaningfully unite with another group only using a language they do not understand.

People are in various stages of receptivity

We need to plan our mission work accordingly. Where there is little receptivity, a holding operation needs to be going on with a few personnel. Where receptivity is great, send the workers into the harvest field in great numbers. The main reasons for receptivity are social.

Reaction: A very useful concept. This really is the place for sociological factors - in preparing people for openness to the gospel. McGavran should be read carefully at this point.

Not all factors are social. Prayer is needed for opening hard hearts.

Redemption and lift

When a person becomes a Christian he changes away from his immediate contacts in society. Redemption is used to describe the changes that occur through him becoming a Christian and joining a church. Lift is used to describe those changes which result from him benefiting from missionary activity - education, medical work, employment, etc. These both tend to take the convert out of his circle of friends and contacts - to which he is the most effective witness. Mission policy must work to ease this problem and converts be encouraged to witness while contacts are still close, to cross the bridges while they are still there.

Reaction: This is a valid way of coming to Christ. If the Holy Spirit can work in one heart, he can work in many in a kinship group at once - especially if they usually make decisions in this group way. See Acts 16 vs 31-34.

But, great care needs to be taken and McGavran is not sufficiently careful here. Sociological factors may make a whole people receptive but that only allows them to hear the Gospel sympathetically. No one becomes a Christian solely for sociological reasons! Only when they are touched in the heart about their sin and turn to Christ are they saved. Any other way produces crowds of nominal Christians. By all means let there be group decisions of this sort, but let each person be examined for his own personal faith before baptism.

General response

McGavran has done the Church a good service by pointing out the sociological dimension of witness and church life and growth and we must take this into account. It is important to understand this dimension for the purposes of witness, communication, judging receptivity and redemption and lift. God works in and through social needs and pressures.
   Two great dangers are present with McGavran's theses.

1. He applies social factors beyond the above mentioned usefulness to the extent that people are seen to come into the Church just for social reasons. This is confusing and damaging to the Church. Social factors produce receptivity, they do not produce Christians without a personal response to the Gospel.

2. Homogeneous unit churches are unbiblical and generally to be discouraged. Numerical growth is not necessarily the most important measure of church growth, and yet McGavran elevates it to the position where it becomes the test of whether a church is growing at all.

Sociological factors are not the only, or even the most important factors in church growth. Spiritual issues such as urgent prayer, a return to a full, clear Gospel, radiant, believing Christians and preachers, and the outpouring of the Holy Spirit, historically have been crucial factors that triggered church growth in its full sense. Often in such cases, social factors have also been used by God in preparation for His blessing. McGavran notes all this but does not integrate it well into his overall presentation.
   We have not covered all of McGavran's presentation above, only those elements which were particularly significant for our purposes in this chapter. Other elements in his presentation are Indigenisation, Frontier Mission Work, City Ministry and Revival.

Selected bibliography:

D.A. McGavran, *Understanding Church Growth*
  Eerdmans, Grand Rapids, Revised Ed. 1980

Eddie Gibbs, *I Believe in Church Growth*
  Hodder and Stoughton, London 1981

Orlando Costas, *The Church and its Mission*
  Tyndale, Wheaton, 1974, pp 87-152

Harvie M. Conn, Ed, *Theological Perspectives on Church Growth*
  Presbyterian and Reformed, New Jersey, 1977

C. Rene Padilla, *Mission Between the Times*
  Eerdmans, Grand Rapids, 1985, pp 142-169

16.
Mission to Unreached Peoples

"The total number of the unreached, for the next thirty years at any rate, will increase...............year by year". D. McGavran.

This is also known as Hidden Peoples Mission Work or Frontier Mission Work. It is an emphasis which has captured the imagination and programme of Evangelicals in the last 20 years or so and must be seen as a significant refocussing of the missionary task for our generation.

History of an idea

The modern missionary movement began with William Carey going out to unreached people, mostly on the coast of the newly opened land of India. Many followed him to the African and Chinese coasts.

The next stage can be seen to begin with Hudson Taylor who left the Christians and the work on the coasts and pressed inland, founding the China Inland Mission. Soon other interior missions followed such as Africa Inland Mission, Sudan Interior Mission, Regions Beyond Missionary Union and Unevangelised Fields Mission.

Other societies coming later, combined the two approaches. Qua Iboe Mission, for instance, established a work on the coast and then moved inland up the Qua Iboe River in West Africa. Gradually, churches were founded and grew up. Soon the view began to be voiced that all nations had now been evangelised, that there was a church in almost every third world nation and so there was no need to send any more missionaries to the unevangelised. The task was now only to support the church in those lands. There were calls for missionaries to withdraw altogether. Such was the prevailing view in the 1950s and 1960s in many quarters.

This thinking was upset by two men who refused to think and work on the basis of political nations and showed instead that in each modern nation there are many peoples and that national boundaries are very artificial. Some of these peoples groups are without witness at all, so we need to send missionaries to them as unreached peoples.

Donald McGavran - a missionary in India noted carefully the complicated mosaic of different tribes and castes, and saw that many were without a church of their own. He defined the homogeneous unit as the target for mission and he interpreted the 'all nations' of Luke 24 v 47 as 'all ethnic groups'.

Cameron Townsend - a missionary in Guatemala, realised that while the trade languages of Latin America all had Bible translations, many tribes were without the scriptures in their own local language. He also saw people as tribal, ethnic groups. The Wycliffe Bible Translators, which he began, go into unreached tribes and translate the Scriptures.

So the deadlock was broken and the peoples group concept became a vital conceptual tool which showed us how we should be focussing our efforts in primary evangelistic missionary work. This approach was adopted at the Lausanne Conference of July 1974 after a keynote message by Ralph Winter. A World Consultation on Frontier Mission was held at Edinburgh in 1980. Mission Advanced Research Centre (MARC) has begun a collection of data on the unreached peoples groups of the world. Worldwide Evangelism Crusade (W.E.C.) publish *Operation World* by Patrick Johnstone, which also gives carefully collated information and this society has made the evangelism of unreached peoples groups the main thrust of their work. Many other missionary societies are now seeking out these 'hidden people' for the Lord.

Winter's presentation

Ralph Winter was a colleague of McGavran at Fuller, but left to found the United States Centre for World Mission in California. His address at Lausanne gave an important impetus to the concept

Mission to Unreached Peoples

and should be consulted by the student. This can only be a very brief presentation of his ideas.

Cross Cultural Evangelism

Like McGavran, Winter rejects artificial national boundaries and sees peoples groups as the unit to be dealt with in missionary work. Whereas all nations may have a church; within those nations - and even across the borders of nations - many peoples of distinct language and culture are not reached at all. It follows that we still have to cross these cultural boundaries with the Gospel and this is the most urgent task of the Church today.

The Terminology of Cross-Cultural Evangelism

Unreached people are at various cultural distances from the missionary. Winter defines the different types of Evangelism/Missionary Work that needs to be done as follows:

E 0 Evangelism - is Christians reaching out to those nominal Christians in their own churches.

E 1 Evangelism - is Christians reaching out to those non Christians that speak their own language and belong to their own people's groups. E 0 and E 1 evangelism is the easiest type because of the lack of cultural obstacles.

E 2 Evangelism - is the missionary reaching out to those non Christians who are of a different people's group but have a similar language, culture and customs.

E 3 Evangelism - is the missionary reaching out to those non Christians who are of a totally different culture and strange language - that is those at a maximum cultural distance. This is the hardest evangelism of all, yet it must be done first so that there will come into being a church in that people's group which will then be able to reach out to its own people in the much more effective E 1 type of evangelism.

The terminology can be illustrated like this:

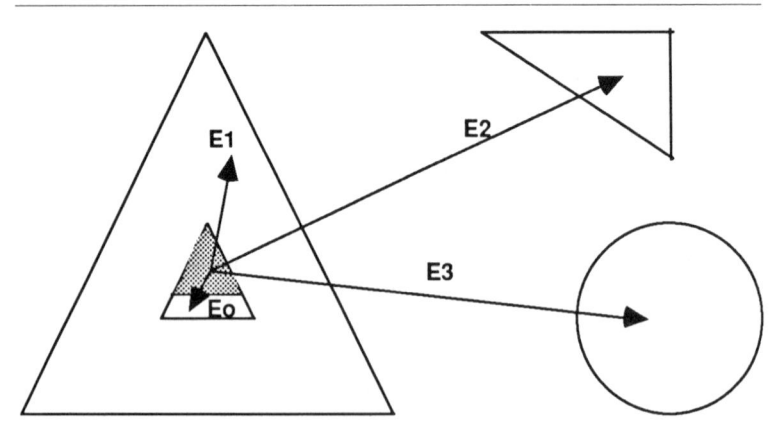

Now this terminology corresponds roughly to our Lord's distinctions in Acts 1. "You will be my witnesses in Jerusalem and all Judea (E 1) and in Samaria (E 2) and unto the uttermost part of the earth (E 3)".

For a Christian in a church in the United Kingdom, E 0 would be talking to his friend in the church who is not yet saved; E 1 going door-to-door in his street; E 2 preaching the Gospel in Southern Ireland and E 3 going as a missionary to Thailand.

The task in each nation can then be analysed in terms of the proportion of each different type of evangelism still to be done so Nigeria as a whole may look like this.

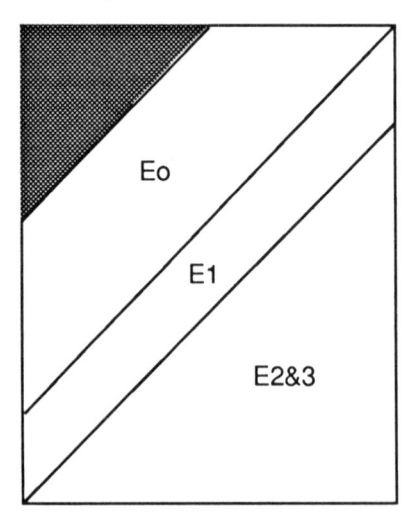

The extent of cross cultural evangelism still to be done

The task is only about half done according to Winter. Here is his own diagram in a simplified form.

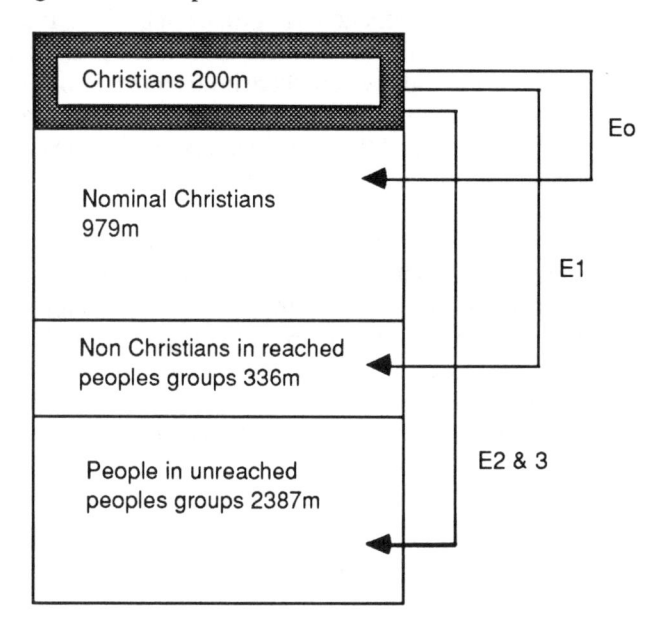

```
┌─────────────────────────────────┐
│  Christians 200m                │──┐
├─────────────────────────────────┤  │  Eo
│                                 │◄─┘
│  Nominal Christians             │
│  979m                           │
│                                 │──┐
├─────────────────────────────────┤  │  E1
│  Non Christians in reached      │◄─┘
│  peoples groups 336m            │
│                                 │──┐
├─────────────────────────────────┤  │  E2 & 3
│  People in unreached            │◄─┘
│  peoples groups 2387m           │
│                                 │
└─────────────────────────────────┘
```

It follows from these statistics that the main thrust of missionary work must now come in E 2 and E 3 evangelism - cross cultural, pioneer missionary work to unreached peoples. But is this what is happening? Not at all! In fact over 90% of all western missionaries are working in and with churches or engaging in E 1 evangelism. We need a radical reorientation of missionary work today!

Assessment

The basic facts and presentation are very moving for anyone who longs to see Christ's kingdom extended. However, we must not be carried away on emotion but sit down and carefully assess the ideas.

A lot depends on definitions. What is a peoples group? Is it a people that are ethnically and linguistically distinct, or can it also be a different caste or clan or age group or type of worker within that ethnic group? Winter would define it in the second sense, others in the first. Are Chinese taxi drivers in Chicago, or young people in a provincial town, people's groups? This radically affects the statistics.

How do you assess whether a people's group is unreached? Some have taken as unreached all groups with less than 20% Christians, others as those where there is no witness at all among that people. Others as those where there is no church strong enough to reach out to their own people. Again, your definition radically affects your numbers - and this in turn alters your strategy. For a good discussion of this issue, see Glen Myers book listed below (Appendix).

As we saw with our analysis of Church Growth ideas, teaching and nurturing of Christians is also vitally important. This in turn contributes to missionary work since a true, well taught church should be a missionary church to its own people and beyond. Nevertheless, the reservations expressed above are not enough to destroy the overall pattern of the presentation. It should remain before us as a guide and spur to reaching out to those still unreached today.

Selected bibliography

Ed. Allan Starling, *Seeds of Promise*
World Consultation on Frontier Missions, William Carey Library, Pasadena, 1981

Ralph Winter, *The New Macedonia*
William Carey Library, Pasadena, n.d. (His address to the Lausanne Conference).

David Frazer Ed., *The Church in New Frontiers of Missions*
MARC, Monrovia, 1983

Glen Myers, *The World Christian Starter Kit*
W.E.C., Gerrards Cross, 1986, Appendix

Harvie M. Conn Ed.,*Reaching the Unreached*
Presbyterian and Reformed, New Jersey, 1986

17.
Social Responsibility as Mission

"Church members who deny in fact their responsibility for the needy in any part of the world are just as guilty as those who deny this or that article of faith". W.A. Visser't Hooft.

800 million people (one fifth of the population of the world) lack the basic necessities of life. Forty thousand children die every day who would not die if they had good food and good basic health care. (UNICEF Figures, 1986). Many across the world lack human rights and are tortured and killed by oppressive regimes. War is always raging in at least one part of the world at any time.

What is the Church's mission in this situation? Is it only to preach the Gospel so men and women will be born again and so heal the world? Or is it also to minister to the victims of this sin by relieving human need, and doing works of mercy? Or should the Church go further and seek to remove the causes of human need and suffering, seeking justice and political freedom and fairness. Is the Church only there to dress the wound, or should she also try to stop the person who is wounding the people?

These issues have become the subject of much debate among Evangelical missiologists in the last 20 years and tension still exists today. This chapter seeks to give some background information and outline an approach to the issue.

Conflicting attitudes

Until recently there had been a complete polarisation of views between the Evangelical and Conciliar (WCC) movements on this issue.

The older evangelical view

Mission is evangelism. Missionaries are evangelists. Evangelism was often described in terms of proclamation of the Gospel. Many saw medical and educational work as not central to the missionary task and solely as a platform for preaching the Gospel. But this can and should be criticised on two counts.

1. It is not the historic evangelical position. Wilberforce and Shaftesbury in the last century worked with one hand for social justice and mercy, and with the other for the preaching of the Gospel.

2. It is not an adequate response to the command of Christ. As Stott has pointed out, one version of the Great Commission (John 20 v 21) says, "As the Father sent me, even so send I you". Jesus healed the sick, bound up the broken-hearted and cleansed the temple as well as preached the Good News of the Kingdom.

This extreme viewpoint should be regarded as a healthy reaction to the "social gospel" of the liberal theologians at the turn of the century, but it went too far.

The World Council of Churches view after 1967

Up until the preparatory work for Uppsala in 1967, Mission and evangelism were roughly equated in WCC circles. Then the word took on a new meaning. It is the mission of God in this world (Missio Dei) with which we must be concerned. He is at work bringing "shalom" - harmony, peace and justice. He uses men and women inside and outside the churches in this task.

Christians must look at the world and seek to serve according to its present social needs. This is to participate in God's mission. This also can and should be criticised on two counts:

1. Mission should be used to describe what God sends his people into the world to do. That squares with the root meaning of the word. God is at work in many ways, in providence and

common grace, in society. Mission is what he sends his Church to do.

2. This view leaves little room for evangelistic concern. The apostles went out on mission primarily because people were perishing without Christ, and they preached the Gospel so people could be saved.

This viewpoint is another demonstration of the principle that where the Gospel is not clearly held, mission work becomes confused.

Views of relationship

In the last twenty years or so, many Evangelicals have seen the need to bring together what is right in both viewpoints, and to discuss the relationship of Evangelism and Social Responsibility within missionary work. In this section, we will look at three attempts, each containing much truth, but all of which I believe to be inadequate.

1. Social Action as a means of Evangelism
In this case, the winning of converts is the purpose of all the work. A mission hospital exists so that you can preach to the patients. Food is given out so that people will want to hear. The work is not simply an expression of the love of Christ, it is the bait on the hook.

This is an unhealthy attitude which borders on hypocrisy. It often produces 'rice Christians'. In any case, if conversion is the aim of medical work then historically it has not been a very efficient form of evangelism.

2. Social Action as a part of Evangelism
J. Hermann Bavinck holds this view. Medicine and education are more than "a legitimate and necessary means of creating an opportunity for preaching,.....If these services are motivated by the proper love and compassion, then they cease to be simple preparation and at that very moment become preaching". In other words, deeds and words go together. You preach the love of Christ by dressing the tropical ulcer.

This is surely true. Many have come to Christ because they have seen and received his love from others. But is that the main *justification* for dressing a tropical ulcer? Or is it because it causes pain if not dressed? The Christian nurse does not so much say, "Now let me preach the love of Christ to this man by dressing his ulcer". She says, "Oh you poor man, let me help you, whether you see Christ in this deed or not".

3. Social Action and Evangelism are distinct but equal
This view is expressed by Ronald Sider. Social action and evangelism are both part of the mission of the church to the world but neither depends on the other. They each stand in their own right. Nor can you say that one is more important than the other since Jesus seemed to spend at least as much time healing the sick as preaching the Gospel.

We should agree that both are distinct aspects of ministering the love of Christ - of being Christ to the people. Each has a separate and adequate justification for its importance in Christ loving the needy through us. Yet, as the Lausanne Covenant says, "In the Church's mission of sacrificial service, evangelism is primary". This is for two reasons. *Firstly*, because the Church will only be able to serve the world if it has born again members. Evangelism creates the Church which serves the world. *Secondly*, evangelism concerns a man's eternal destiny, social action only helps the temporal body. Saving Grace is therefore man's greatest need. Only the Church brings that to a person. Communists can feed the hungry. Of course, we rarely have to choose and generally, as in the ministry of Jesus, the two are inseparable.

A biblical approach

1. Useful Models We have already seen how it helps us to look at the missionary task as the love of Christ poured out to a needy world through us. This has led us to see the need to love the body as well as the soul and include social, medical and other work in our definition of mission work. In the writer's view this is easily the best model of missionary work. There are two other models that are popular these days and which help us in our understanding of the relationship between evangelism and social action.

The missionary brings salvation. Now in the Bible, salvation is often used of physical rescuing from distress, pain and injustice -

Social Responsibility as Mission

particularly in the Old Testament. In Africa and other parts of the Third World where the relationship between soul and body, natural and spiritual is seen as much closer than in a Western culture, the Gospel is expected to bring wholeness and have an interest in the body's and society's pains. Great damage is done to the Biblical concept of salvation, however, if the greatest stress is not laid on reconciliation with God, by Christ,as salvation. The benefits of Christ's death and resurrection will only come to the physical world in fullness when the end of the age dawns (Rom. 8 vs 19-25). To equate salvation with political liberation is missing the main point.

The missionary brings The Kingdom. The Kingdom is the rule of God. Jesus preached that, in him, the Kingdom had come. The signs of the coming of the Kingdom were the preaching of the Gospel and the spoiling of the Kingdom of Satan by exorcism, healing, conversion, etc. These signs announce the arrival of the Kingdom and anticipate the final coming of the Kingdom in all its fullness at the end of time. As his Kingdom is extended into the Kingdom of Satan, it seasons it with salt and enlightens it (Matt. 5 vs 13-16). It is clear that there is more to bringing the Kingdom than preaching the Gospel. Along with the preaching goes defeat of Satan and his enslavement of people in suffering. Yet we must insist that the Kingdom only fully comes to a person (or to put it another way, a person only enters the Kingdom) when he acknowledges Jesus as Lord and King.

2. Relationship We have already agreed that evangelism and social action are distinct and stand on their own, but (as has been reinforced by our discussion above), evangelism is the priority. How do the two relate? We can show the relationship in a diagram:

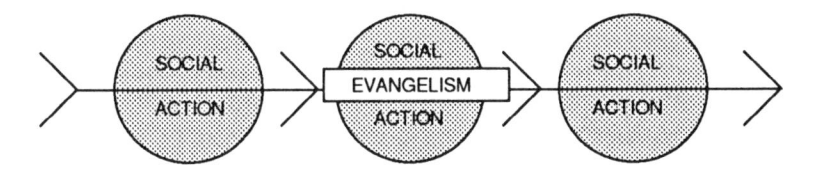

Firstly, social action can go before Evangelism in the sense that it can open closed doors, break down prejudice and be a bridge across which the Gospel can pass. We can move from a people's "felt needs" to their spiritual needs. But it must be for love and compassion not in order to create the bridge. Even if no bridge were created we would want to do it anyway.

Secondly, social action can go along with evangelism as its partner - like the two wings of a bird, as in the ministry of Christ, words explain the works, works demonstrate the words. Both are an expression of love.

Thirdly, social action will follow evangelism as its natural consequence. As people are converted and taught to observe everything the Lord commanded, they will show their faith by their works and feed the hungry and visit those in prison and clothe the naked. Indeed, one of the reasons why Christ gave himself for us was "to purify for himself a people of his own who are zealous for good deeds". (Tit. 2 v 14).

The extent of the church's social responsibility

We have concluded that social action is a valid part of missionary work - though not the primary task. That is evangelism. But to what extent should the Church get involved? All seem agreed that healing the sick, feeding the hungry, ministering to problems and distress are right forms of service. Historically, most missions in Africa have included education in the list and it has usually been a valuable way of helping a society.

Many today wish to go beyond the traditional forms of service, to look beyond individuals who suffer, and try to do something about the people and structures which cause the suffering. Such social changes often necessitate political involvement, hence the saying, "love that is not political is not love" (Camara). This is where many Evangelicals draw back, but such drawing back is not necessary if care is taken. Our Lord spoke out against the rulers who burdened the people, the prophets spoke out against injustice, many great Evangelicals have worked in and through the political system to achieve Christian aims such as the abolition of slavery and child labour. But we can only get involved in ways that are Biblical and honouring to God. Violence against a government is not one of those ways.

Mission is the Church sent into the world to love as Christ loves, to extend his rule of love. It will mean the Church firstly and most importantly preaching the Gospel of Grace and urging people to get right with God. It will also mean the showing of compassion to the physically needy, in a Biblical and effective way.

Selected bibliography

Lausanne Occasional Papers No.21, *Evangelism and Social Responsibility*
    LCWE/WEF, Wheaton, 1982

Ronald J. Sider, *Evangelism, Salvation and Social Justice*
    Grove Books, Bramcote, 1979 (1977)

John R W Stott, *Christian Mission in the Modern World*
    Falcon Books (CPAS), London, 1977 (1975)

Waldron Scott, *Bring Forth Justice*
    Eerdmans, Grand Rapids, 1980

Bruce J. Nicholls Ed., *Evangelism and Social Responsibility*
    Paternoster (for LCWE & WEF), Exeter, 1985

PRACTICE
The Missionary and the Churches

18.
The Missionary Call

"God is at work in you, both to will and to work for his good pleasure". Paul. (Phil. 2 v 13).

The most popular question when speaking on missionary themes is, "What is a missionary call?" It is often asked by serious men and women who realise the importance of the Great Commission and want to know their part in the work. Is it to stay and pray and give? Or is it to go?

We should begin with the certainty that missionary work is God's work and he selects the personnel. Can we know clearly whether we have been selected? Of course. God does not leave his servants in darkness when he wants them to work for him. But how can I know what the Lord's will is for *me*? That is the subject of this chapter.

Many mistakes have been made in this area. Some would-be missionaries have waited for a wonderful vision - almost a voice from heaven - before moving. Others have lightly volunteered their services as if it depended on them. Both approaches have been encouraged by some societies and both are wrong.

What is a missionary call?

It can be conveniently seen in four parts. Although God deals with each person individually, we would expect each part to be present in every missionary call.

BURDEN	GIFTS
CHURCH	CONFIRMATIONS

The burden

If the Lord wants you to go, the first thing he will probably do is lay a great burden on your heart for the work. The Lord may disturb you with the state of the lost without the knowledge of Christ, or the state of the churches in areas where it so struggles that you cannot tell whether it is living or dying. He may lay on your heart a burning desire to have the joy of extending Christ's Kingdom, to see more and more people come under His Lordship.

He may challenge you with the needs of the mission field compared with those at home. Someone who was burdened in this way by God once said, "If you see ten men carrying a tree trunk, nine at the light end and one at the heavy end and you want to help, to which end will you go?" The heavy end with few workers is still the mission field today.

The need is not the call, but if the Lord has burdened you with the need it may well be an indication that he is calling you. If he has burdened you with a particular aspect of the great need, it may be an indication that he wants you to help meet it.

The gifts

Another thing the Lord will do for a man or woman he wants on the mission field is prepare him or her for the work by giving the necessary gifts and character. You will know whether you are called to preach the Gospel by whether the Lord has given you the gift of preaching. You will know whether the Lord wants you to do it on the mission field by whether he has made you the sort of person who should be a missionary. You will need such things as a fit body, genuine spiritual life, experience in service, adaptability, the ability to endure hardship, emotional stability and so on. See the chapter on "The Missionary - what sort of person?" Often you are not the best judge of whether the Lord has equipped you for the work, so rely on the opinions of some godly men and women who know you and know about missionary work.

Church

It is not God's usual way to call a man or woman without the involvement of his church. In fact, not one missionary called in the New Testament is recorded as being sent on his own initiative alone. In every case the church, as a body or in the shape of a senior missionary, was involved in the call. Barnabas went to Antioch because his church sent him there. Both Paul and Barnabas went out from Antioch as a result of a joint decision by the church leaders guided by the Holy Spirit. In Paul's case, about nine years had elapsed since his personal call to be a missionary.

There are rare occasions when the candidate's church is so out of touch with the will of God that this is impossible. Jeremiah was in a similar situation. But in these cases there are almost always other godly people who will confirm your judgment.

Missionary work in the third world will only go forward as the church there gains a burden and, like the church in Antioch, sets aside its best people for the work. Expect the church's acknowledgement and official sending if you are called by God.

The confirmation

Other factors often play a significant part in a person's call to missionary service. God's arranging of circumstances to make it possible for you to go is important. Obstacles will be removed. You will be accepted for service, support will come in. The particular form and place of service will often be indicated in this way, (Acts 16 v 7).

Dreams, visions and convictions from the Holy Spirit were used by God in New Testament times and also today. They can initiate a call to service or can come later as confirmation. But they must always be tested and only accepted and followed when other Biblical signs are in agreement.

The Lord sends peace in your heart after prayer, and particularly after a decision before him that you will go. This coming of peace is an inner witness of the Spirit that you are in the Lord's will.

If you are already in full-time service

It is often the Lord's way to call a man to the preaching of the Word of God or evangelism in a home situation and then some years later, call him out to work in a missionary situation. This happened in New Testament times. It may well be the best way forward for mission work in, for instance, Africa or Asia today for the church to send some of its best experienced preachers to the mission field.

The same constituents of a call will be present for such a man. However, he may like to see his call in two parts; the call to the full time service of preaching the Word of God and then, specific guidance as to where he should exercise that ministry. When God has gifted and called a man into his ministry, he can place him in a home church for a number of years, guide him to the mission field for, say, ten years and then move him on to yet another sphere of service. The church is world-wide. Every minister has to ask himself, "Now where does God want me to discharge my ministry?" and be willing to be sent anywhere, like a soldier on active service. You can see the specific guidance of God operating in the life of Paul a number of times - (e.g. Acts 16 vs 9-10).

What should I think if I am called?

1. Read this chapter again prayerfully, asking the Lord to show you what to look for in your heart, life and church.

2. Set aside a part of your daily prayer to offer yourself entirely to God to go where he sends you and to do whatever he wants of you.

Willingness is necessary for guidance. Ask him daily for a clear knowledge of his will.

3. Read missionary biographies for inspiration and other missionary books for understanding of the work.

4. Work for the Lord where you are. If you are not interested in doing this then you are certainly not called to work for the Lord elsewhere. It will also be of help to you. It will reveal something of the type of gift you have and so the type of service you can be expected to be called to.

5. Begin to talk to people about it. Discuss it with godly men and women who know you. Talk to your church officers. Make enquiries from your mission board or from missionary societies. Explore possibilities. Boats can be steered only when they are moving. Get moving and God will steer you.

Selected bibliography:

David J. Hesselgrave, *Planting Churches Cross-Culturally*
   Baker, Grand Rapids, 1980, pp 137-143

Oswald J. Smith, *The Cry of the World*
   Christian Witness Productions, Kaduna, 1985 (1959) pp 91-96

J. Herbert Kane, *The Making of a Missionary*
   Baker, Grand Rapids, 1975, pp 1-36

19.
The Missionary - What sort of Person?

"The church (at Antioch in Acts 13) sent the best of its leadership group". David J. Hesselgrave.

Not all Christians have the necessary qualifications for missionary work. Nor indeed need they, for God calls us into different work according to our ability. However, the study of missionary qualifications is important for two reasons:

If a missionary society, board of missions or church is to accept a person then they need a standard of suitability.

Such considerations are part of the evidence of a call of God. God only calls suitable people - that is, those he has made suitable.

The qualifications are high and rightly so. The missionary is at the cutting edge of the work of Christ's Church. He is in the front line in the spiritual battle and the best soldiers should be sent to the front. It is a tragedy if, in a bout of enthusiasm, a church or society sends out unsuitable people. In such a case, they will add to the problems rather than further the work.

Nevertheless, no one since Christ has been a perfect missionary. No one will have all the qualifications. Where a candidate is missing one or more of the traits mentioned below, then we must ask two questions:

Is this lack sufficiently balanced by a greater strength in another area?

Is this lack in such an important area that it will be deadly to the Lord's work? Such areas are to be found especially in the spiritual and parts of the psychological sections.

It cannot be stressed too strongly that we need to know all the facts before a decision is taken and all possible means are to be used to obtain them; detailed forms, interviews, referees, talking with those who know the candidate well. When the facts are known, the decision must be made by balancing two truths - God wants the best, and God uses us despite our weakness.

Physical qualifications

Good, consistent, all round health is important because life on the field is generally harder physically than at home, especially if there are major differences in climate and way of life between the area the missionary comes from and the one he goes to. In such cases, small problems of health become larger; chronic (regular) sickness can become a serious interference. Also, medical facilities in some areas are harder to come by. It is good to insist on a proper medical examination before a person is sent.

Academic qualifications

High academic achievement is not necessary for all forms of missionary service. Peter and John were judged to be unschooled and ordinary men - but they had been with Jesus (Acts 4 v 13). However, down through the ages, great missionaries have often, like Paul, been outstandingly academic people. A consistent policy of looking down on academic achievement when selecting missionaries greatly harms the church that is founded and this has been a general weakness of the Faith Mission movement of this century. Similarly, a policy of only accepting those with high academic qualifications will ensure that you miss some of the people the Lord wishes to use.

All missionaries need three things:

General intelligence (trained in the university or not).
A good working knowledge of the Word of God and related disciplines.
A firm understanding of missionary principles and practice.

The Missionary - What sort of Person?

Specialist missionaries will need other academic training related to their ministry. For instance, Bible translators need a good understanding of the Biblical languages and linguistics; Bible College lecturers need more training in theology.

Psychological qualifications

Every person is a unique personality and there are many different types of people working successfully on the mission field. Nevertheless, certain characteristics should be present and all involved with missionary candidates should look for them carefully. If available, a psychological examination, written or oral, can be used.

1. Emotional Stability The missionary faces many pressures and frustrations, often without adequate Christian fellowship. He needs to be mature and stable, a rock to lean on rather than one who always leans on others.

2. Adaptability Some people are so set in their ways that they find change almost impossible. But the missionary will be going to a strange area and strange people with strange ways. He will have to fit in. He is the one to change life, not them.

3. Ability to endure hardness His standard of living will probably drop. This is very noticeable for westerners coming to the third world, but it also applies to much indigenous missionary work. The hours are long and the work is difficult. Not all can endure separation from family and people.

4. Patience The person who expects results in a short time will often leave the field in a short time if they don't come. What is needed is people who say, "I am committed to this situation, to gently and patiently serve this people for 5, 10 or 20 years."

5. Drive, Enthusiasm, Initiative These are not all exactly the same thing, but they are usually found in the same people. We are thinking of a person who can throw himself into the work, plan, execute, follow up, keep at it with energy and ingenuity until it is done. Most missionaries are leaders.

6. A spirit of co-operation This is the ability to get on with others, whether they be indigens of the area in which you work or other missionaries who may be from a very different background to your own. The best missionary is usually a peaceful person who can work in a team.

Spiritual qualifications

The missionary must be a person of God. Weakness in other areas can be allowed him if this is the case. The greatest and most essential qualifications for fruitful missionary work are spiritual.

1. Genuine Conversion As John Wesley found, it is a terrible mistake to go to the unconverted without being born again yourself.

2. Conviction of Call A missionary must be able to say, "I am here by the will of God doing what he wants me to do". Once the missionary can no longer say that, he may as well go home. Indeed, he probably will, because there is nothing to keep him there on the field in times of hardship and disappointment.

3. A strong, disciplined devotional life Daily private prayer, Bible study, worship, all must be part of the habits of his life. In his home town the missionary is in a church he knows and loves. Christian friends and helpers, the regular preaching of the Word, all help to sustain his spiritual life. On the field, many of those supports may be absent. Who ministers to the missionary? Who checks up on his spiritual life? The duty often falls on himself.

4. Love The Lord wants missionaries with love or not at all (1 Cor. 13). They must be able to say with Paul, "We loved you so much that we were delighted to share with you not only the Gospel of God but our lives as well". (1 Thess. 2 v 9). The people you go to will forgive you much if they can see that you love them.

5. Experience and Success in Christian Service A candidate must first prove at home that the Lord can and does use him to win souls or to build up his church. How can he do these things successfully in a difficult place if he cannot do it among his own people?

A note on missionary preparation

Missionary training and preparation has not often been adequately thought out or practised in the past. It is mostly recently that colleges are running courses giving full and comprehensive training for the work. As in any other calling, good training greatly increases efficiency and usefulness. It can be seen as consisting of four parts: the Word, the life, the culture and the profession.

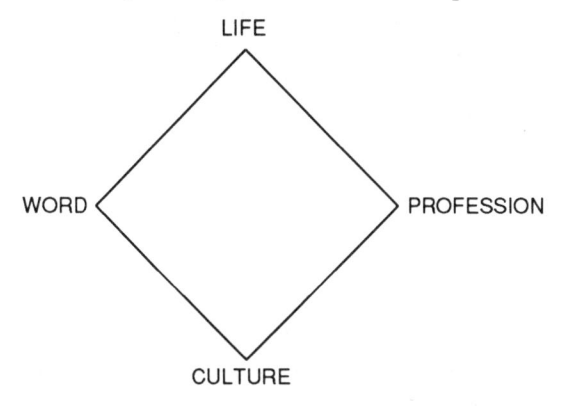

```
           LIFE
            /\
           /  \
          /    \
    WORD <      > PROFESSION
          \    /
           \  /
            \/
         CULTURE
```

1. Word The missionary should be trained in the scriptures at the highest academic level that he can handle. It is a complicated, highly educated world today. He needs to know the Word clearly and comprehensively, deeply and accurately. He should know what to preach, how to preach it and how to defend it. All related subjects which bear on this task are also valid areas of study. Almost always, this will mean some years in a Bible or Theological College.

2. Life The missionary requires serious training in his Christian life, particularly those areas which have a strong effect on his usefulness and service. Training in discipleship - (living a completely committed life in a practical way); growing in a life of faith and prayer - (knowing how to serve God in a spiritual way); seeking fullness of the Holy Spirit. These were the characteristics of the missionaries in Acts who turned the world upside down. (Acts 4 v 8, 6 v 5, 11 v 24).

One of the best ways for many to find training in such areas is through short term service with such organisations as Operation Mobilisation or in some of the special retreats and discipleship courses run by such people as Calvary Ministries, Nigeria. Rarely is an ordinary Bible College training adequate in this area.

3. Culture For a missionary to be effective, he has to change from being an ethnocentric person (one with only the experience of his own people and way of life) to become a bi-cultural evangelist. He needs a basic understanding of cultural factors and social structures, how they change from people to people. He needs to be taught how not to bring his own "cultural baggage" with him when he goes with the Gospel; how to adapt. He needs tools for language learning. One of the best ways to acquire these things is, after some classroom work, to have exposure to another culture, even for a few weeks, as a short term missionary assistant.

4. Profession This applies, of course, to the specialist missionary such as the doctor, teacher, printer, etc. It also applies to the "tent maker" who uses a profession to enter a closed or difficult land. But in an important sense it also applies to the missionary as a missionary - that is his profession and he should understand the job and how to perform it. In other words, he needs proper training in missiology, of which this book is designed to be a beginning.

Selected bibliography:

J. Herbert Kane, *The Making of a Missionary*
   Baker, Grand Rapids, 1975, pp 37-7)

Lyman E. Reed, *Preparing Missionaries*
   William Carey Library, Pasadena, 1985

J. Oswald Saunders, *Spiritual Leadership*
   Moody Press, Chicago, 1967

Pius Wakatama, *Independence for the Third World Church*
   Intervarsity Press, Illinois, 1976, pp 83-94

Dr. Marjory F. Foyle, *Honourably Wounded*
   MARC Europe, London, 1987, pp 84-89

20.
Incarnation

"If Jesus Christ be God and died for me, then no sacrifice can be too great for me to make for him". C.T. Studd.

The best model for a missionary is Christ himself. In John 20 v 21, Jesus says to his disciples, "As the Father has sent me, even so send I you". The Biblical pattern is for each missionary to leave his home and *incarnate* himself into the life and community of the people he comes to serve.

The theological base

In coming to earth from heaven, Christ crossed the ultimate cultural/social barrier and his incarnation provides the pattern for our own. It was of two parts (Phil 2 vs 5-8, especially verse 7).

Emptying It is a matter of theological dispute as to exactly what Christ left behind. Certainly he left those things which belonged to heaven rather than earth which would make his life of suffering service impossible.

Taking He took the form of a servant and was made in the likeness of men. He became like one of us. He was not in any way an especially privileged man, but a simple carpenter with a poor life.

It was an immensely costly thing to do because the greater the cultural distance, the greater the personal cost. Why was it necessary? For our salvation which *had* to be accomplished this way. The temptations of the devil after our Lord's baptism can be seen as tests of just how far he was willing to walk this road of incarnation. It was also essential for proper communication between God and man.

Billy Graham tells a story about a man who came across an ant hill severely damaged by a wild animal. The man felt compassion and stooped down to help but his clumsy fingers only did more damage and hurt the injured ants all the more. Then he thought, "If only I could become an ant, then I could help them as one of them and teach and show them the way out of the mess they are in". That is what Christ did for us and what missionaries have to do with the people to whom they are sent.

Paul's method is clearly explained in 1 Cor. 9, and is incarnation: "To the Jews I become a Jew, to the Greeks I become a Greek. I become all things to all men in order that I may win some" (paraphrased). This has also been the method of the best missionaries down through the ages.

The practical outworking

The only attitude to take in this section is one of humble admission of personal failure and a great carefulness not to become the judge of others as to how they serve their master. (Rom. 14 v 4).

1. General Attitudes The missionary must determine in his mind, "I will leave behind my old way of life and adopt the way of life of the people to whom I am sent". He will want them to say, "Yes, he's one of us, let us listen to him". This will involve respect for the people, appreciation of their way of life, never looking down on them or drawing unfavourable comparisons with your own land or people. It will involve a desire to enter into their life, to understand it and live it, to be able therefore to empathise. It will mean in other words, a love for the people that, like Christ, is a giving of yourself to them. It will show itself in such little things as food. To accept a people is to accept their food. To reject their food is to reject a people. You will also take delight in taking time to greet the people in the way that shows acceptance and respect in their culture.

2. Language and Culture Learning In order to get into the mind of the people, know what they are thinking and know whether you are really communicating, mastery of the indigenous language is important. But it is not just of use as a tool for understanding. To learn another person's language is a gesture of acceptance and

Incarnation

commitment to them - in other words, part of incarnation among them.

The culture and customs of a people also need careful learning, again, for understanding, but also to avoid offence by the things you do or the way you dress or what you say. It is perfectly acceptable to accept a gift with the left hand in England. It is offensive to do so in most parts of Nigeria. You need to know.

3. Finance More often than not, a missionary comes from a people richer than those among whom he works. What must he do? Like Christ, he should not hold on to the difference in standard of living, but empty himself and, as far as possible, live like them. Any serious financial difference will get in the way of the message. If you project a picture of comfort and affluence you will cut yourself off from the poor to whom you must preach the Gospel - except when they come to your door for financial help! You will be seen as the bringer of riches rather than the bringer of the Gospel. A family person who is a missionary must strike a balance between the suffering of his family and the poverty which brings closeness to the poor. Single missionaries are not so torn apart.

4. Housing The missionary in most situations, but especially in evangelistic work, should live in an average type house right in the middle of the social life of the area. He must *not* create a mission compound but live with the people he seeks to understand and reach. You as a missionary must see how they live in the intimate details of everyday life in order to understand them. They must see how you live so that you can preach by life as well as by word. You must have neighbours and friends whom you can win to Christ. Your house must be close to them and the sort of house they can come into and feel at home, not as if they are in a strange foreign place. Usually this will mean rented accommodation is the best.

5. Taking Time Christ could have come for six months, died and returned, but he chose incarnation which for him meant about 33 years! When crossing linguistic and cultural distances with the Gospel, think in terms of a *minimum* of three years to become useful. It will take at least this long to learn the language sufficiently, understand the people and have a reasonable time of ministry among them. After that, the longer you stay the more useful you are.

This has to be balanced with the need for church planters to move on as soon as a viable church is functioning (see previous chapters).

Paul's movements in Acts were more rapid because he never had to cross a linguistic barrier. There will come a time when the church planter will need to move on to a new area of the same people and begin again.

In many other ways, we can follow Christ's incarnation. Indeed if we do so, we open ourselves to letting Christ minister to the people through us - if we incarnate ourselves among our people for him.

Selected bibliography:

Phil Parshall, *New Paths in Muslim Evangelism*
    Baker, Grand Rapids, 1980, pp 97-126

Orlando Costas, *Christ Outside the Gate*
    Orbis Books, New York, 1982, pp 3-20

21.
Missionary Preaching

"God was pleased through the foolishness of what was preached to save those who believe."
"How can they hear without someone preaching to them?"
Paul, (1 Cor. 1 v 22 and Rom. 10 v 14.)

Preaching the Gospel is the central act of missionary work. Paul said, "Woe is me if I do not preach the Gospel." Ultimately, a missionary is a person with a message, who is charged with communicating that message to people, on God's behalf.

Where and when?

Preaching is not just the act of one person standing in front of a congregation. The preaching of the Gospel takes place whenever and however the message is faithfully communicated. Many missionary situations can make use of the well tried pattern of four simultaneous approaches; public preaching, private speaking, literature and a godly life lived among the people. All this being backed up by earnest prayer for the success of the message. It can be represented thus:

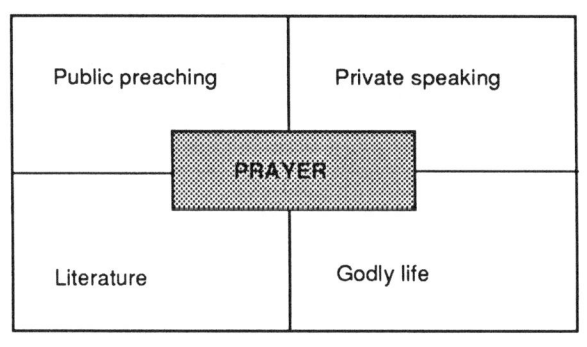

Public preaching	Private speaking
PRAYER	
Literature	Godly life

In some areas of Africa, Asia and Europe there are constraints on public preaching. In other situations, house to house is not productive. We need to research carefully, plan prayerfully and be flexible and ready to change as things become clearer to us - all in order to fit the approach to the situation. Other opportunities for communicating the Gospel such as access into schools, use of the mass media, mobilising Christians from nearby areas to help - all these can be considered and fitted into the plan. The aim is a clear and persuasive communication of the Gospel to every person in the area.

1. Public Preaching This is the method most often recorded in the Acts of the Apostles. The right place needs to be chosen. If a church building is already in existence, don't automatically think of using it for Gospel preaching. It is our duty to go to them, not sit down and invite them to come to us. The best places are where many people gather and have time to stop and listen.

The correct style for the people is also important. It need not be a typical 'sermon' such as is preached on a Sunday morning in church. Paul reasoned with the Jews. There can be dialogue and questions. It need not be cluttered up with all the other things that are done on a Sunday, such as hymns, prayers, offering. It may be that the best way in one situation will be to sit down with the chief in his compound and explain the Gospel to those who gather. If you have the resources, the staging of a play to commence the preaching may or may not be culturally acceptable.

2. Privately (usually including from house to house) Wherever people sit, work or talk, you can go to them, sit with them and tell them of Christ. But a visit to a man's own house is often very welcome. With what aims? Partly to minister to the needs of that home. Maybe someone is sick and you can pray for them, or sad and you can encourage them, or without food and you can bring them some. Show the love of Christ that is in your heart for them.

Mainly, however, it is to put to them the Gospel, to discharge your responsibility as a carrier of the Word. A further connected aim would be, after a few visits to an interested home, to found a regular Bible study in the home where you can open the Word to them and perhaps their neighbours in a situation where they do not feel threatened or pressurised. Four or five such home Bible Studies in a village can soon lead to the formation of a church.

3. Literature If a piece of literature is put into the hands of the person you have been talking to, he can read and study and think about the Gospel until you call on him again. You can then easily recommence the conversation by asking him what he thought of the literature. Alternatively, it can be used to announce who you are and what you bring, so they are ready to hear you when you come. It is necessary that the literature is produced to the highest quality in order to demonstrate the importance of the message. It should be in the vernacular if possible but simple English may be preferable in some situations.

4. A Godly Life It is of little benefit to visit people from a long way away. They don't know you and you don't know them. How can they make an estimate of your message without knowing you? You must choose to live with them and mix with them. Then you must take great care to show them Christ in your life as well as your words. Bring Christ to them by word and deed.

How?

In this section we are talking about the nature and content of the message the missionary brings to the people. It must be:

1. Theological In a non Christian situation there is inevitably a lot of theological foundation work to be done before the Gospel can be clearly perceived and taken in. Looking at Peter's and Paul's sermons in Acts we see a lot of theology introduced. The doctrines of God, man, Christ, judgment, salvation, all needed to be explained properly.

2. Clear At the heart of it all is a way of salvation which the preacher needs to be very clear about in his own mind, and be able to put it clearly and simply to the people once they have understood the great doctrines at the heart of the Gospel.

Having known of his sin and the character and wrath of God, and his coming in judgment, a man must *repent.*

Having known of Christ, who he is and how he came and died for sinners as a substitute, a man must put his *faith* in Christ as his own Saviour.

Having known of the Lordship of Christ, and the cost of becoming a Christian, he must *commit* himself totally to Christ as his Lord.

What a man must know	What a man must do
His sin, God's holiness, judgement	Repent (turn from his sin)
Who Christ is and what he did - especially the cross	Put his faith in Christ as his Saviour
Christ is Lord. There is a cost to pay	Commit himself totally to Christ as Lord - become a disciple

3. Contextual Paul only had one Gospel, but the *presentation* of that Gospel varied with the context in which he preached. To the Jewish monotheists in the synagogues, Paul began from the special revelation of the Old Testament which they accepted (Acts 9, 13, 17). To the pagans of Lystra, he began with explanations about himself, then God and creation (Acts 14). To the philosophers of Athens, he began with their form of worship and their own writers (Acts 17).

People's understanding varies. Their open sins are not the same everywhere. The consequences of sin show themselves differently in different situations. In every society, the cost of declaring as a Christian will be different. The point of contact is where people are, their beliefs and their felt needs. Begin there and lead them on to what they should believe and what their deepest spiritual needs are. So you can say to a drunkard, "Christ can free you from this". You can say to a tribe in fear of witchcraft, "Christ can protect you" and then go on to explain more about Christ.

On the whole question of saying things in such a way that a people of a different culture can understand our message, see the chapter on Cultural Anthropology.

4. Costly Never make it easy to become a Christian. Our Lord, when crowds followed him, usually spoke of the cost of being his disciple. There has to be a decision to take up the cross and the inquirer must know what the cross will entail before he comes to Christ. Unless you make it clear, you fill your church with nominal or weak Christians.

Calling for a response

There comes a time when people should be asked to decide. How do you handle this? Let it be:

1. Not too early Time needs to be given for sufficient teaching, and for it to be understood. Reflection and the working out of the cost will often take time. If much of Christian teaching is coming to people for the first time, we need to be patient. However, if a person presents himself as seeking Christ, it is often wise not to delay him or put obstacles in his way.

2. Without pressure The practice of an "altar call" is usually confusing and counter-productive in many missionary situations. People go forward easily with little knowledge of what they are seeking or should seek - especially if they have been stirred up emotionally by a clever speaker. An invitation to see you privately, either there and then or by you visiting their house the next day, avoids many problems.

3. With an Act of Repentance True repentance is often focused in an act of renunciation. In pagan societies it must be burning of personal ju ju or idols (or if they are owned by the clan, giving them up). For an unjust rich man like Zacchaeus it will mean returning a lot of money to many people. In a Muslim culture it may mean the acceptance of Christian baptism which cuts the ex Muslim off from his former religion - often to great personal danger.

4. Deciding Together People can come to Christ in families or groups. Let us present the message to families as a whole, even villages as a whole. But then, if there is a collective response, let us personally interview each inquirer to see that it is also an individual decision.

Selected bibliography:

J. I. Packer, *Evangelism and the Sovereignty of God*
    I.V.P., London, 1961

David J. Hesselgrave, *Planting Churches Cross-Culturally*
    Baker, Grand Rapids, 1980, pp 199-230

Michael Green, *Evangelism in the Early Church*
    Hodder and Stoughton, London, 1970

22.
Church Planting

"The primary mission of the Church and, therefore, of the churches is to proclaim the Gospel of Christ and gather believers into local churches where they can be built up in the faith and made effective in service thereby planting more congregations throughout the world." David J. Hesselgrave.

The Church is both the agent and the goal of mission. We do not go out for decisions for Christ only, but to plant churches where there are none. The purpose of the church is threefold:

For God's sake. To make real the aim of God in mission - to have a people for himself to worship, serve and live in fellowship with Him.

For Our sake. To give the converts the mutual support and encouragement of a group of similar people. Humans are gregarious and God made us that way. He fulfils this in his Church.

For the Lost's sake. So that the church formed can become the agent of mission to those around initially and also to the ends of the earth.

So, every mission must sort out its ecclesiology, but this has rarely been done in advance. The attitude has been that we will preach the Gospel and think about the rest later.

The steps from evangelism to church are set out in the Scriptures:

Peter preaches - Acts 2 v 14
People respond - v 41
Baptism - v 41
Founding of the church - vs 42-47 - which involved teaching, fellowship, sacrament, prayer, worship, outreach by example (favour of the people) and the preaching of the apostles.
As a result other churches were founded e.g. Antioch - Acts 11 vs 19-26

Those newly founded churches, in turn, sent out missionaries - Acts 13 vs 1-3

Baptism

This has already been discussed in Paul's missionary methods but here we would emphasise a few things. Baptism is the rite of entry into the Christian Church. In N.T. times usually it was the occasion of the person's entry into both the visible and invisible Church since it was the time when the person called upon Christ for salvation, in and through the sacramental act. (See Beasley Murray, *Baptism in the New Testament*). However, in church history, the outward act and the inward act of faith have been usually separated - by infant baptism for example in the Presbyterian tradition, where it is assumed that the act of faith will come later and so complete the baptism - or, by many missions in Africa where the separation has been the other way, since they required a long time of teaching after faith in Christ before the candidate was ready for baptism.

Ideally, personal conversion and baptism should be as close as possible provided a clear understanding of the Gospel and of baptism is present. Teaching comes afterwards. In tribal situations we must be particularly clear with the people as to the distinctiveness of Christian baptism. It is so easy for them to see it as another rite of passage into the spiritual protection of a religious society (church), with little of the Biblical emphasis.

The church in native dress

The traditional way of solving the problem, "How do we plant a church in a missionary situation?" is just to copy the church where the missionary came from. So Anglican missionaries plant Anglican churches in the heart of Africa which use the 17th century prayer book of the U.K. church. Methodists plant Methodist churches, Presbyterians import Presbyterian orders of services, church structures and even the style of church buildings!

Why not? These things (outward, practical matters of church polity and form) are the creation of a history in a particular society. They fit in the U.K. or U.S.A. because of the history and society which created them. There are reasons for their use there. There are not the same reasons for their use in, for instance, Africa. Africa has a different history and society. We would expect other forms to fit better. Assuming that we will reproduce our own churches is denominational arrogance - Is our way really the best for all people in the world? It may well be blocking the freedom of the Holy Spirit to create a people as he wishes in that context.

Unity can exist within cultural plurality. Other peoples need not be made to bow to our way of doing things. Pressures from the converts themselves to follow exactly the foreign ways should be gently discouraged, despite the honourable reason that it means for them a complete break with their perhaps evil and pagan past. Mission founded churches today are suffering great losses because of this misguided policy in the past, and today's missionaries must be very careful not to repeat the mistakes of the past.

Three models which have been historically influential

1. The Three Selfs Formula
Henry Venn and Rufus Anderson articulated these ideas in the 19th century and Roland Allen is also associated with the view. Every missionary church must be moved, as soon as possible, towards being:
  Self Governing
  Self Supporting
  Self Propagating
This was the policy adopted by many missionaries, at least in name, and it is embodied in the constitution of many churches. A number of criticisms have been raised against it.

It has become an outdated 'catch phrase' that everyone agrees with but is put into practice in very different ways. "We are working towards this...." can mean anything.

It doesn't work well in all situations. It is easily applied when many are converted quickly, but when growth is very slow, to apply it rigidly would be to cripple the witness in that area.

It has not necessarily led to church growth. Continued outside help has speeded up church growth in certain situations.

Above all, all three selfs can be true, but you still do not necessarily have an indigenous church. The organisation can be Western, the hymns, the order of service, the church in all its details can be Western, self governed, self supported and self propagated by Indians!

Realisation of its limitations has led missiologists to seek another definition. Related to this formula, and of great historical and practical importance is *The Nevius Method* set out in Korea in 1890. Its four principles are:

Each Christian should "abide in the calling wherein he was found", support himself by his own work, and be a witness for Christ by life and word in his own neighbourhood.

Church methods and machinery should be developed only in so far as the Korean Church is able to take responsibility for the same.

The Church itself should call out for whole-time work those who seemed best qualified for it and whom the church was able to support.

Churches were to be built in native style, and by the Christians themselves from their own resources.

2. *The Indigenous Church* This goes beyond the three selfs and talks of the moulding of the church according to the culture of the people. Daniel C. Hardin defines it: "An indigenous church is a church in which God, Christ and the Holy Spirit, in contact with people of a particular cultural setting, give rise to a Christian body that is outwardly and uniquely moulded by that culture over a fixed framework of fundamental Scriptural doctrine" (*Mission, A practical approach to church sponsored mission work,* William Carey Library, Pasadena, 1978, p 184.).

A very useful model of indigenisation is provided by Kraft - "a Dynamic Equivalence Church" - see "Dynamic Equivalence Churches" *Missiology* vol. 1 No. 1 (Jan 1973) pp 39-57.

Notice that this approach is anchored in two things - the New Testament and the local culture, and it is a dynamic interaction under the power of God between these two. Forms of liturgy, types of leadership, methods of witness and loving, buildings, behaviour, ways of teaching, all are determined by the basic principles laid down in Scripture and by any specific commands of Scripture - and also by what is right and good in the way the people do things so long as this does not go against the principles and commands of Scripture. Of course, the more homogeneous the church is, the more distinctive it can become. City culture, as a melting pot of cultures is more elusive and the missionary often has to be much more pragmatic.

This indigenisation can only occur if real understanding of and respect for the culture is present in the missionaries, and leadership is given early on to the converts before patterns have hardened. A word of warning: It is this area which has produced much controversy in the past between missionary and missionary. No one interprets either the culture or the Scripture exactly the same way on every specific issue of church life. Humility and love are very important.

3. Contextualisation For the background to this relatively new way of looking at the issue, see Bruce Nichols 'Contextualisation' and the article in the Dictionary of Evangelical Theology edited by Elwell. It is a term which originated in the W.C.C. but the force of its thrust has been recognised by many Evangelicals outside the conciliar movement. It is more concerned with the particularisation of the Gospel in a situation than of a church, but it is relevant to the concerns of that newly planted church.

Whereas indigenisation was mainly concerned with adaptation into a culture and the communication of the Gospel in that culture, contextualisation requires a concern for social, political and economic questions. Salvation involves salvation of the society as well as of the individual and the new church should be concerned and involved. Another distinctive is that while indigenisation historically hardly concerned itself with institutions, thinking only of the local church, contextualisation is very concerned that institutions reflect the cultural, economic and social situation in which they operate. This is of especial importance in Bible Colleges and ministerial training.

Indigenisation should remain the dominant model for our church planting, but it must be overlaid with a concern that the new church be salt and light in the society in which it is planted.

Setting up the basics

It is the duty of the missionary to see that a functioning church is left

Church Planting

as a result of his work. For this, he has to pay attention to at least three main areas.

1. Meetings All Christians need and desire fellowship and while this will be found in their day to day contact in each other's houses, the meeting of the church where all come together is very important. We need to determine the **time** of the meetings, and here there must be real flexibility and sensitivity to the local situation. Because one pattern works in the South of a country, it does not follow that the same days and times are right or convenient in the North. The **place** of meeting must be decided. The early church had no built meeting places but existed in people's houses or in the open air for hundreds of years. However, we need to examine the situation. In some lands it is often wise to build as early as possible since it gives a validity and respectability to the church which assists greatly in evangelism.

The **type of building** must be one that is suitable for the climate and area and will probably be modelled on traditional buildings of the area. The interior will reflect the desire for simple fellowship in worship and around the word of God. It must not mean that the house meeting is abandoned entirely since this is a good evangelistic tool also. The **contents** of the meeting are determined by the New Testament as to its basics - worship, prayer, ministry of the Word, reading the Scriptures, giving, singing of hymns and psalms and sacred songs. In Corinth there was also an open time of worship where spiritual gifts were exercised. However, the order and structure of the meeting is not laid down and one can and should adopt an indigenous pattern. Hymns and songs need not only be translations!

In New Testament times it seems that the Lord's Supper was given a prominent place in every weekly gathering on the Lord's day. This should be set up with indigenous leaders presiding so it can go on as a part of that local Church's life if the missionary or distant pastor is absent.

2. Leaders The first leaders are appointed by the missionary, although if his denomination does not give him that authority, it should be done with his advice. Rules include:

   Plurality of elders, to avoid autocracy.

Gifts need to be present - of administration and teaching.
Moral character must be suitable, see 1 Timothy and Titus.
Training of leaders is very important - see our Lord with the twelve disciples.
A rudimentary system of church government is inevitable within which the leaders will operate.

Historically church government systems, while claiming direct Scriptural support have all arisen out of both local culture and the New Testament. There is no reason to avoid this if the Scriptural requirements are upheld. Let it be simple.

3. Teaching This is part of the Great Commission and falls initially on the missionary who brings the Gospel to the people. It was an important part of the life of the Old Testament people of God and of the life of the New Testament church (Acts 2 v 42, 2 Tim. 2 v 2). We need to teach new churches often and regularly in a clear systematic pattern with definite aims to cover so much in a particular time. The drawing up of a teaching programme for a new church is one of the most important things to be done. The natural style of the teaching needs to be appropriate. The Western pattern of 40 minute sermons may not be appropriate or useful. Catechisms may be of great benefit, but not Western ones, rather your own which will be relevant and in tune with the people.

The content must likewise be selected with care, to be faithful to the whole counsel of God and also to be useful to the people as they try to be obedient to the Word in their specific situation. Special care needs to be taken if doctrines and concepts are being taught in a language for the first time that what you think you are saying is what they are receiving. (See the chapter on Cultural Anthropology.)

It will include:

The great doctrines, beginning with those related to salvation so they can understand what has happened to them.

The Scriptures themselves, the background, study methods, etc. so they can read them themselves with profit.

Obedience to Christ, Discipleship and the Christian life. This will involve personal holiness, the cultivation of personal fellowship with God, giving, witness and missions.

Finally then, the task will come full circle and you can guide the new church to become a missionary church.

Selected bibliography:

David J. Hesselgrave, *Planting Churches Cross Culturally,*
   Baker, Grand Rapids, 1980

Edward R. Dayton and David A. Frazer, *Planning Strategies for World Evangelism,*
   Eerdmans, Grand Rapids, 1980

Charles H. Kraft and Tom N. Wisley, Ed., *Readings in Dynamic Indigeneity,*
   William Carey Library, Pasadena, 1979

Monica Hill, Ed., *How to Plant Churches,*
   MARC Europe, London, 1984

23.
The Missionary as Servant of the Church

"The terms, 'sending' and 'receiving' churches are becoming meaningless, for we are all sending and we are all receiving."
H. Rowdon.

The pattern for a person called to evangelistic and church planting missionary work is the founding of churches and then, as soon as they are established, a handing over of authority to the church officers and a moving on to found other churches. But this is not the only type of missionary work. Medical mission for example is also a bringing of Christ's love to the people and this operates under a different pattern. Of the greatest importance today is the missionary who comes to serve an already established church - usually by Bible teaching. That is the subject of this chapter.

His place and justification

This is to be found in Biblical examples and in the theology of the church.

Timothy, Titus, Crescens, Tychicus, were all sent by Paul to various established churches to help build them up and put things in order (2 Cor 8 v 23, 2 Tim 4 vs 10-12, 1 Tim. 1 v 3, Titus 1 v 5). Apollos is another good example and in 1 Cor. 3, Paul describes the difference between his job and that of Apollos. "I planted the seed, Apollos watered it". Paul himself fulfilled this function at Antioch for some years (Acts 11 vs 22-26). There were also many other wandering prophets and preachers serving the churches in the early days of the Church. Not all were orthodox (2 Jn. v 10).

There is only one Church. The Lord gives gifts and gifted people to his Church as a whole, not just to any one local congregation

(Eph. 4 v 11, cf. v 4). He is free to move them where he wishes. When there is one group of churches lacking Bible teaching and another group of churches with Bible teachers enough and to spare, he has often called some from the first area to go where the need is. The churches must be in fellowship with each other, care for each other and meet each other's need (2 Cor. 8 vs 13 and 14).

Stages in mission - church relationships

Historically, the role of the missionary serving an already established church has been full of problems as both the missionary and the church try to sort out their changing roles. Geoffrey Dearsley of S.U.M. and Ralph Winter of U.S.C.W.M. have produced a descriptive table of changing Mission/Church relationships which is reproduced below with comments. It is not what *should* happen, it is rather what generally *has* happened.

STAGE	ROLE OF THE MISSIONARY
PIONEER	E2 and E3 Evangelism on his own initiative. Language learning and translation
PATERNAL	Sets up institutions ad runs them all. Supervises the National churches. Has the major voice in all church conferences. Assigned to work by the mission not the church.
PARTNER-SHIP	Invited by National church and assigned to work by them. His opinion is often asked but not always followed. Still in charge of projects involving money from abroad. Never serves as pastor.
PARTICI-PATION	Always works under National leader. His work budget directed by the National church.

STAGE	ROLE OF NATIONAL LEADERS
PIONEER	No National leaders at first. Selected men begin training and help the church.
PATERNAL	In charge of local churches. In charge of locally raised funds but not those from abroad. Votes in church conferences. Leadership roles but usually under a missionary.
PARTNER-SHIP	All administration and leadership at National level. In charge of most monies even from abroad. Requests and assigns missionary personnel.
PARTICI-PATION	Administers all funds, local and foreign. Adminsters all former missionary work. Sets up and runs its own mission agency.

This is by no means an ideal pattern. Stage two (Paternal) is only to be considered when we have a highly institutional mission. Even then, it is doubtful if it is wise. If the mission must run the institutions at this stage, need it also run the churches? See the Nevius method mentioned in the lecture on church planting. If a paternal stage lasts a whole generation then much harm can be done to a church.

All four stages may be present in one "mission field" at one time since some areas may be in different stages of development.
Different types of missionary are needed for different areas of mission work. The pioneer must be an independent minded person with initiative. Such a person is often frustrated in the quiet co-operation needed during the partnership stage.

Mission/Church tensions almost always come in the transition between the paternal and partnership stages.

Teaching in context

It is seldom realised how complicated is the task of the missionary

Bible teacher if it is done properly. In fact, usually he has to be at home in three different cultures. He must know the cultural background of the Old and New Testaments in order to understand the Word clearly. He will need to know Western culture in which theology has grown for so long in order to discern what is of God and what is simply the adaption of the message for the use of the Western church. He will need to know the culture of the people to whom he is to minister, its way of understanding, those concepts which do not translate well, its areas of special need to which he must minister. If he is a Third World missionary working in a different culture to his own, the task is even more complicated. It is arrogance to simply take the notes of the teaching he has received and pass the contents on to the people. He must create a truly indigenous theology; totally faithful to the Word of God, but packaged in a way suited to the people. This was New Testament methodology.

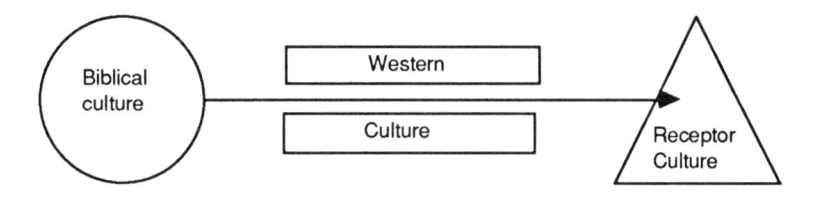

The Bible teacher should also contextualise his method of teaching. A Western style seminary or college may not be the most useful way to train leaders. Some form of Theological Education by Extension may be preferable, or even an apprentice-disciple situation such as our Lord employed with the twelve disciples. The Bible teacher will need to work on literature at the level of the people and any other teaching tool which he can use to discharge his trust.

Serving the church is a most difficult and delicate job but the partnership which develops between church and missionary is often that of mutual loving respect *if that is the missionary's own attitude to the churches.* In such a case the relationship is greatly useful for the Kingdom.

Selected bibliography:

Pius Wakatama, *Independence for the Third World Church*,
    I.V.P., Illinois, 1976

David J. Hesselgrave, *Planting Churches Cross-Culturally*,
    Baker, Grand Rapids, 1980, pp 401-421

J. Andrew Kirk, *Theology and the Third World Church*,
    I.V.P. Illinois, 1983

W. Harold Fuller, *Mission - Church Dynamics*,
    William Carey Library, Pasadena, 1980

Melvin L. Hodges, *The Indigenous Church and the Missionary*,
    William Carey Library, Pasadena, 1978

24.
The Sending Church

"No church which is involved in true mission ever remains unchanged." D. Bosch.

Mission is most importantly the sending of people called by God from a church to found another church in a different people. We have explained elsewhere that this is a very simplified view of things, but it is essentially correct. It follows that there is a whole area of mission practice which relates to the sending church. If the task of missions is to be done, then we must create *missionary churches* to do it. We can divide this into three areas: interest, prayer and finance.

Interest

There are few churches of which we can say that they have enough missionary interest, and those few that have need to constantly be kept interested in the work of missions. We need to set goals and use means.

What are we trying to achieve?

1. Knowledge We want a church which knows the necessary facts. You cannot be interested in what you do not know. The facts about missions are by themselves very moving. We need to teach the understanding of what mission is and the detailed, relevant facts about the fields, the missionaries and the needs.

2. Attitudes We want a church which takes the correct attitudes. What are these? You can see them set out in the chapter on motives for engaging in the task. Let me emphasise here the need for hearts of love for the lost, which can only be created by the Holy Spirit, and the church seeing itself as a part of a worldwide body with a world wide task.

3. Enthusiasm Knowledge and attitudes must issue in enthusiastic work, support, prayer etc for missions. How? One means is to be enthusiastic yourself. Enthusiasm is infectious. Don't fall into the trap of condemning people all the time for their lack of interest, rather, set them an example, Present the facts and pray for the right attitudes.

How do we achieve these goals?

1. Concentrate on the Leaders, the Elders, the Youth Fellowship and Women's Fellowship leaders, the committees. These are the opinion formers of the church. They must be captured for missions first.

2. Use the Pulpit. If you are the regular preacher, this is easy. Preach about mission. The Bible is full of it.

3. Organise. See that the information is there, including information about rallies, etc. Find missionary books and sell them. Organise trips to conferences. See that there are ways they can give to mission, and times and places where they can pray for mission. If you are a large church you can appoint a missionary secretary and a missionary committee.

4. Pray. God moves the hearts of the people by prayer based on the preaching of the Word of God.

Missionary prayer

Paul pleaded in the strongest language for his churches to engage in prayer for his work. (Romans 15 vs 30-33).Why is missionary prayer so vital?

1. It gives the correct perspective on the work. It is not by clever plans, but by God's spirit. If you pray, you demonstrate such an attitude.

2. Historically. It has always been by prayer that the great missionary advances have been made. We can think of the prayers of the Moravian Brethren which soon issued in the great missionary work of those people, or the Friends Prayer Bands of India which soon turned into sending agencies for hundreds of missionaries.

3. It gives those who pray a share in the missionary task. (Rom. 15 vs 30-33). They actually join in the struggle, the spiritual struggle which is missionary work.

What should be the content of our prayers? Four things stand out in Scripture:

For workers to be sent to the field (Matt. 9 v 37).
For guidance who to send, where to go (Acts 13 vs 1 & 2).
Success of the message (Eph 6 vs 19 & 20, Col. 4 vs 2-4, Matt. 6 v 10).
Protection and help for the missionaries (Rom. 15 v 31)

In particular, there ought to be a regular supply of information from the missionary on the field to the church. Then those who sent him can pray for specific needs and rejoice when prayers are answered. Western missionaries generally send a duplicated 'Prayer Letter' to those who pray for them regularly. It is necessary for us to encourage missionary prayer at four levels in any local church.

Individually. In a person's own daily prayer time. He or she can remember a missionary each day, keep his latest letter, or a list of specific needs in their Bible for easy reference.
In the family devotions of our members.
In a prayer cell of a few people deeply interested in missions. Such a cell can meet regularly to receive new information and pray over it together.
In the church as a whole in its prayer meetings and in the prayers of the church services. Every weekly prayer meeting a person can be responsible for mentioning some missionary needs for prayer.

Finance

If a missionary is sent from a church, then that church has a special responsibility to help in his support. If it is a large church, it can do it alone. If it is a small church, then it needs the help of its fellow churches. The ideal situation is that a missionary feels accountable to his local church in every way, still under the direction of his elders. And the church in turn feels responsible for the missionary in prayer and giving. But whether a church has its own missionary or not, it ought to plan seriously to give to missionary work. At the end of the year, the accounts of a church, or group of churches should show that a good proportion of income has gone to the evangelisation of the world. After all, we received the Gospel because someone gave to missionary work.

Money is important in that it is one of the means God uses to send missionaries. Missions run on money. Paul was not always supported and in fact he went without guarantee of support and at times had to work to support himself. Nevertheless, his work went more easily when he had support. Philippians chapter 4 is a good example of a church participating in mission by giving (vs 10-20). Of course, all the principles involved in giving to the Lord in general apply to missionary giving, and we do not have space to go into them here, except to mention three areas.

1. Generosity (2 Cor. 8 vs 1-16). This is a generosity which is to the point of self-sacrifice, the going without for the sake of others and the Lord's work. It is based on the fact that our Lord has given all for us and we have this opportunity to respond in gratitude, and follow his example.

2. A necessary life-style. We cannot give to missions as we ought and maintain our present way of life. Now, for the genuinely poor and needy, God only asks the widow's mite, but most of us could live in a cheaper, simpler way and this would release funds for the work. This principle applies also to churches. Towers, new buildings where the old one will serve, are not necessary. Missionary work is! Let our churches be simple, just enough to allow us to worship God, and let the money remaining be released for building the kingdom.

3. Practical arrangements. Money needs to be collected. How do we do it? - in accordance with the general principles of giving - secretly, regularly, in proportion to our income. Let us only take money for missionary work if it is freely given without compulsion and if it is given only to spread the kingdom, and not to make a person seem generous and good in the eyes of his fellows. Many missionary societies do not appeal for money. They prefer to plead with God rather than plead with people (2 Cor. 8 vs 3 & 4). Our duty is three-fold: it is to (a) make the need known, (b) Give the opportunity for people to give if they so desire, (c) Pray that God will meet the needs of the work.

"God's work, done in God's way never yet lacked enough money".
                                                            Hudson Taylor

Selected bibliography:

Jim Graham, "Restoring Mission to the local church" in *We Believe in Mission.*
    Ed. John Wallis S.T.L., Bromily, 1983, pp 145-159

Harold H. Rowdon, *Turning the Church Inside Out*
    BMMF, UK, 1982.

Graham Cheesman, *The Church and Mission*
    Q.I.F., Belfast, 1985

Postscript

Now that you have come to the end of this book, I hope you can look back on an enjoyable time of study. But Mission Studies is not only for the head. It demands a response. You should not leave this book uncommitted, but rather dedicated to the work of extending the Kingdom.

Maybe this book has been like the opening of a window to you, so now you can see a whole new area of obedience to the Lord for your life. After all, Jesus said, "If you love me, keep my commandments", and our studies have centred around the Great Commandment to take the Gospel to every creature. Now you know. More light brings more responsibility.

How will you get involved? A few may go, though not all are called. All can pray and you should make a point of getting information and praying regularly in private and public for missions. All can give even a little. If you are in an influential position in Christ's Church you can stir up others to become aware and involved - especially in your preaching. Some may like to take Mission Studies further and read deeper. This course is only an introduction.

Whatever you decide God wants you to do, for the rest of your life, be a Christian deeply involved in God's missionary work across the world.

Appendix 1
Resources for Further Information

Periodicals

There are four, large circulation, important journals on Missiology.

Missiology published by the American Society of Missiology - a grouping of Evangelicals, Catholics and Conciliar missiologists. It contains much of great value.
Missiology, 616 Walnut Avenue, Scottdale, PA
   15683-1999, U.S.A.
   Issued quarterly $15 U.S. per year.
International Bulletin of Missionary Research published by the Overseas Ministries Study Centre, roughly as broadly based as Missiology. A greater emphasis on scholarship and research. Perhaps the best of them all.
   I.B.M.R., Overseas Ministries Study Centre
   6315 Ocean Avenue, Ventnor, New Jersey 08406, U.S.A.
   Now distributed in UK by Paternoster Press. Issued quarterly
   $14 per year.
Evangelical Missions Quarterly published by the Evangelical Missions Information Service (linked to the two big Evangelical Missions Associations in the U.S.A., the Evangelical Foreign Missions Association and the Interdenominational Foreign Missions Association.). Purely evangelical, yet a popular approach which doesn't always have sufficient depth.
   E.M.Q., 25w560 Geneva Road, Box 794
   Wheaton, Ill. 60189, U.S.A.
   Issued quarterly $11.95 U.S. per year

International Review of Mission published by the Commission of World Mission and Evangelism of the World Council of Churches. Many articles are written from a fundamentally wrong perspective. Has a very valuable cumulative Bibliography on World Missions by Andrew Walls.
    I.R.M., W.C.C., 150 Route de Ferney, 1211 Geneva 20, Switzerland.
    Issued quarterly $17.50 U.S. per year.

Other smaller circulation periodicals of interest are:

International Journal of Frontier Missions concentrating on Unreached Peoples Missions. Published by USCWM, IJFM, P.O. Box 40638, Pasadena, CA 91104, U.S.A.
    Issued quarterly $15 U.S. per year

Bridging Peoples . A newsletter issued by Lawrence Keyes of Overseas Crusades. Devoted entirely to Third World missions.
    B.P. Box 66, Santa Clara, California 95052, U.S.A.

Urban Mission . A periodical dedicated to news and studies concerning mission in towns and cities.
    U.M. Box 27009, Philadelphia, PA 19118, U.S.A.
    Issued 5 times a year $10 U.S. per year

Useful addresses

Those listed below are only a brief selection. Many others are worthy of inclusion.

Organisations

The Evangelical Missionary Alliance. The British umbrella organisation for evangelical missions. Publishes a bulletin of missionary information.
    E.M.A. Whitfield House, 186 Kennington Park Road,
    London SE11 4BT, U.K.

Missions Advanced Research and Communications Centre. A division of World Vision International especially concerned with research.
    MARC, 919 Huntington Drive, Monrovia, California 91016, U.S.A.

United States Centre for World Mission. Devoted especially to Unreached Peoples missionary work, it publishes a number of magazines and houses the William Carey Library publishing house.
    USCWM, 1605 E. Elizabeth Street, Pasadena
    CA 91104, U.S.A.

Lausanne Committee for World Evangelisation. Set up to continue the work of the Lausanne Congress of 1974. It organises consultations, and helps to co-ordinate evangelical mission work. Issues a quarterly publication "World Evangelisation".
    LCWE, P.O. Box 1100, Wheaton, Il. 60187, U.S.A.

Overseas Ministries Study Centre. Organise courses, publishes books and IBMR.
    OMSC, Ventnor, NJ 08406, U.S.A.

Schools of mission

Only a few are listed below:

Westminster Theological Seminary. Specialising in Urban Mission.
    W.T.S. Box 27009, Philadelphia, PA 19118, U.S.A.

The School of World Mission, Fuller Theological Seminary. Specialising in Church Growth and with an emphasis on Cultural Anthropology.
    F.T.S. 135 North Oakland Avenue, Pasadena, CA 91101-1790, U.S.A.

School of World Mission and Evangelism, Trinity Evangelical Divinity School. A seminary with a long and large emphasis on

Mission under Kane, Hesselgrave and Coleman.
T.E.D.S., 2065 Half Day Road, Deerfield, Illinois 60015, U.S.A.

Most Bible Colleges in the U.K. train missionaries. Some have this task as their main objective. Write to "The Association of Bible College Principals, c/o All Nations Christian College and ask for the leaflet *Choosing a Bible Training Course.* Further careful investigation can then be made using the addresses and information from that leaflet.

Four outstanding colleges in this area are:

All Nations Christian College, Easneye, Ware, Hertfordshire, SG12 8LX

Belfast Bible College, Glenburn House, Glenburn Road South, Dunmurry,
Belfast BT17 9JP

Northumbria Bible College, 52, Castle Terrace, Berwick on Tweed, Northumberland D15 1PA

Redcliffe College, 66 Grove Park Road, Chiswick
London W4 3QB

Societies

Missionary Societies exist in their hundreds. For a convenient listing of some of the more important, with addresses, consult *Operation World* by Patrick Johnstone which can be obtained from W.E.C. International, Bulstrode, Gerrards Cross, Bucks, SL9 8SZ, U.K.

Appendix 2
The International Congress on World Evangelisation Lausanne, Switzerland July 1974

Introduction

The congress consisted of 2700 participants (in total, 4000 attenders) from 150 nations across the world. About 50% were from the Third World. All participants were Evangelicals. It was possibly the most significant gathering of Evangelicals from across the world in history.

The congress was called by Dr. Billy Graham after consultation with many Evangelical leaders, as a follow up to the world congress held in Berlin in 1966, but this was a much larger and more representative gathering. The theme was, 'Let the Earth Hear His Voice' and all discussion focussed on how we can fulfil the missionary commission today.

Perhaps the greatest achievement was to launch a new concern and movement of missionary activity and co-operation amongst Evangelicals, but there were at least two other important tangible results:

The Founding of the Lausanne Committee for World Evangelisation. This was set up after the congress to carry on the work of stimulation of evangelism throughout the world. It has an executive committee drawn from all continents, a theology working group, a strategy working group, an intercession advisory group (which designated Ascension Sunday as a day of world prayer for revival and missionary activity and Pentecost Sunday as a day of prayer for world evangelism) and a communications advisory group.

The Lausanne Covenant. This is the document which follows. It was drafted by a committee under the chairmanship of John Stott and approved by the congress as a whole.

It is not an agreed statement so much as a covenant, a binding contract by which the participants pledged themselves to the task of World Evangelisation in these terms and invite others to do the same. However, it is a clear statement of the state of Evangelical missionary theology and provides even today a rallying point for most Evangelicals engaged in the task.

For information on those who consider it inadequately expressed the primacy of evangelism, see Orlando Costas *Christ Outside the Gate,* Orbis Books, New York, pp 158 & 9, although this occurs in a discussion of COWE Thailand 1980. See also Arthur Johnston, *The Battle for World Evangelism,* Tyndale, Wheaton, 1978.

Another important way to look at the congress is to see it as the culmination of a process whereby Evangelicals were working out a coherent and relevant mission theology. Landmarks prior to Lausanne were Wheaton 1966 & Berlin 1966. For more information see Rodger C. Bossham, *Mission Theology,* William Carey Library, Pasadena, 1979, pp 209-255 and Efiong S. Utuk, *From Wheaton to Lausanne,* in Missiology, April 1986 (vol XIU No 2) pp 205-220.

A second international congress on World Evangelisation is to be held in Manila in July 1989.

Selected bibliography:

J. Stott, *The Lausanne Covenant, An exposition and Commentary,*
LCWE, Wheaton, 1984

E.R. Dayton & S. Wilson (Eds), *The Future of World Evangelisation,*
(Unreached peoples, 1984) MARC, U.S.A., 1984

J.D. Douglas (Ed), *Let the Earth Hear His Voice,*
World Wide Publications, Minneapolis, 1975.
(The Conference papers and other material.)

The Lausanne Covenant

Introduction

We, members of the Church of Jesus Christ, from more than 150 nations, participants in the International Congress on World Evangelisation at Lausanne, praise God for his great salvation and rejoice in the fellowship he has given us with himself and with each other. We are deeply stirred by what God is doing in our day, moved to penitence by our failures and challenged by the unfinished task of evangelisation. We believe the Gospel is God's Good News for the whole world and we are determined by his grace to obey Christ's commission to proclaim it to all mankind and to make disciples of every nation. We desire therefore, to affirm our faith and our resolve and to make public our covenant.

The Purpose of God.
We affirm our belief in the one eternal God, Creator and Lord of the world, Father, Son and Holy Spirit, who governs all things according to the purpose of his will. He has been calling out from the world a people for himself, and sending his people back into the world to be his servants and his witnesses for the extension of his kingdom, the building up of Christ's body and the glory of his name. We confess with shame that we have often denied our calling and failed in our mission by becoming conformed to the world or by withdrawing from it. Yet we rejoice that even when borne by earthen vessels the Gospel is still a precious treasure. To the task of making that treasure known in the power of the Holy Spirit we desire to dedicate ourselves anew. (Isa. 40 v 28, Matt. 28 v 19, Eph. 1 v 11,

Acts 15 v 14, John 17 v 6, 18, Eph. 4 v 12, 1 Cor. 5 v 10, Rom. 12 v 2, 2 Cor. 4 v 7).

The Authority and Power of the Bible
We affirm the divine inspiration, truthfulness and authority of both Old and New Testament Scriptures in their entirety as the only written Word of God, without error in all that it affirms, and the only infallible rule of faith and practice. We also affirm the power of God's Word to accomplish his purpose of salvation. The message of the Bible is addressed to all mankind. For God's revelation in Christ and in Scripture is unchangeable. Through it the Holy Spirit still speaks today. He illumines the minds of God's people in every culture to perceive its truth freshly through their own eyes and thus discloses to the whole church ever more of the many-coloured wisdom of God. (2 Tim. 3 v 16, 2 Pet. 1 v 21, John 10 v 35, Isa. 55 v 11, 2 Cor. 1 v 21, Rom. 1 v 16, Matt. 5 v 17 & 18, Jude 3, Eph. 1 vs 17 & 18, 3 vs 10 & 18).

The Uniqueness and Universality of Christ
We affirm that there is only one Saviour and only Gospel, although there is a wide diversity of evangelistic approaches. We recognise that all people have some knowledge of God through his general revelation in nature. But we deny that this can save, for people suppress the truth by their unrighteousness. We also reject as derogatory to Christ and the Gospel every kind of syncretism and dialogue that implies that Christ speaks equally through all religions and ideologies. Jesus Christ, being himself the only God-man, who gave himself as the only ransom for sinners, is the only mediator between God and man. There is no other name by which we must be saved. All men are perishing because of sin, but God loves all men, not wishing that any should perish but that all should repent. Yet those who reject Christ repudiate the joy of salvation and condemn themselves to eternal separation from God. To proclaim Jesus as "the Saviour of the world" is not to affirm that all people are either automatically or ultimately saved, still less to affirm that all religions offer salvation in Christ. Rather it is to proclaim God's love for a world of sinners and to invite all people to respond to him as Saviour and Lord in the wholehearted personal commitment of repentance and faith. Jesus Christ has been exalted

Appendix 2

above every other name; we long for the day when every knee shall bow to him and every tongue shall confess him Lord. (Gal. 1 vs 6-9, Rom. 1 vs 18-32, 1 Tim. 2 vs 5-6, Acts 4 v 12, John 3 vs 16-19, 2 Pet. 3 v 9, 2 Thess. 1 vs 7-9, John 4 v 42, Matt. 11 v 28, Eph. 1 vs 20-21, Phil. 2 vs 9-11).

The Nature of Evangelism

To evangelise is to spread the good news that Jesus Christ died for our sins and was raised from the dead according to the Scriptures and that as the reigning Lord he now offers the forgiveness of sins and the liberating gift of the Spirit to all who repent and believe. Our Christian presence in the world is indispensable to evangelism, and so is that kind of dialogue whose purpose is to listen sensitively in order to understand. But evangelism itself is the proclamation of the historical, Biblical Christ as Saviour and Lord, with a view to persuading people to come to him personally and so be reconciled to God. In issuing the Gospel invitation we have no liberty to conceal the cost of discipleship. Jesus still calls all who would follow him to deny themselves, take up their cross and identify themselves with his new community. The results of evangelism include obedience to Christ, incorporation into his church and responsible service in the world.
(1 Cor. 15 vs 3-4, Acts 2 vs 32-39, John 20 v 21, 1 Cor. 4 v 5, 5 vs 11 & 20, Luke 14 vs 25-33, Mark 8 v 34, Acts 2 vs 40 & 47, Mark 10 vs 43-45).

Christian Social Responsibility

We affirm that God is both the Creator and the Judge of all men. We therefore should share his concern for justice and reconciliation throughout human society and for the liberation of people from every kind of oppression. Because mankind is made in the image of God, every person regardless of race, religion, colour, culture, class, sex or age, has an intrinsic dignity because of which he should be respected and served, not exploited. Here too we express penitence both for our neglect and for having sometimes regarded evangelism and social concern as mutually exclusive. Although reconciliation with man is not reconciliation with God, nor is social evangelism, nor is political liberation salvation, nevertheless we affirm that evangelism and sociopolitical involvement are both part of our Christian duty. For both are necessary expressions of our doctrines of God and man, our love for our neighbour and our obedience to Jesus Christ. The message of salvation implies also a message of judgment upon every form of alienation, oppression and discrimination, and we should not be afraid to denounce evil and injustice wherever they exist. When people receive Christ they are born again into his kingdom and must seek not only to exhibit but also to spread its righteousness in the midst of an unrighteous world. The salvation we claim should be transforming us in the totality of our personal and social responsibilities. Faith without work is dead. (Acts 17 vs 26, 31, Gen. 18 v 25, Isa. 1 v 17, Psa. 45 v 7, Gen. 1 vs 26-27, Jas. 3 v 9, Lev. 19 v 18, Luke 6 vs 27 & 35, Jas. 2 vs 14-26, John 3 v 3, 5, Matt. 5 v 20, 6 v 33, 2 Cor. 3 v 18, Jas. 2 v 20).

The Church and Evangelism
We affirm that Christ sends his redeemed people into the world as the Father sent him, and that this calls for a similar deep and costly penetration of the world. We need to break out of our ecclesiastical ghettos and permeate non-Christian society. In the Church's mission of sacrificial service evangelism is primary. World evangelism requires the whole church to take the whole Gospel to the whole world. The church is at the very centre of God's cosmic purpose and is his appointed means of spreading the Gospel. But a church that preaches the Cross must itself be marked by the Cross. It becomes a stumbling block to evangelism when it betrays the Gospel or lacks a living faith in God, genuine love for people or scrupulous honesty in all things, including promotion and finance. The church is the community of God's people rather than an institution, and must not be identified with any particular culture, social or political system or human ideology. (John 17 v 18, 20 v 21, Matt. 28 vs 19 & 20, Acts 1 v 8, 20 v 27, Eph. 1 v 9, 10 vs 3 & 9-11, Gal. 6 v 14, 17, 2 Cor. 6 vs 3-4, 2 Tim. 2 vs 19-21, Phil. 1 v 27).

Co-operation in Evangelism
We affirm that the church's visible unity in truth is God's purpose. Evangelism also summons us to unity because our oneness strengthens our witness just as our disunity undermines our Gospel of reconciliation. We recognise however that organisational unity

may take many forms and does not necessarily forward evangelism. Yet we who share the same Biblical faith should be closely united in fellowship, work and witness. We confess that our testimony has sometimes been marred by sinful individualism and needless duplication. We pledge ourselves to seek a deeper unity in truth, worship, holiness and mission. We urge the development of regional and functional co-operation for the furtherance of the church's mission, for strategic planning, for mutual encouragement and for the sharing of resources and experience. (John 17 vs 21 & 23, Eph. 4 vs 3-4, John 13 v 35, Phil. 1 v 27, John 17 vs 11-23).

Churches in Evangelistic Partnership
We rejoice that a new missionary era has dawned. The dominant role of Western missions is fast disappearing. God is raising up from the young churches a great new resource for world evangelisation and is thus demonstrating that the responsibility to evangelise belongs to the whole body of Christ. All churches should therefore be asking God and themselves what they should be doing both to reach their own area and to send missionaries to other parts of the world. A reevaluation of our missionary responsibility and role should be continuous. Thus a growing partnership of churches will develop and the universal character of Christ's church will be more clearly exhibited. We also thank God for agencies that labour in Bible translation, theological education, the mass media, Christian literature, evangelism, missions, church renewal, and other specialised fields. They too should engage in constant self-examination to evaluate their effectiveness as part of the church's mission. (Rom. 1 v 8, Phil. 1 v 5, 4 v 15, Acts 13 v 13, 1 Thess. 1 vs 6-8).

The Urgency of the Evangelistic Task
More than 2,700 million people, which is more than two-thirds of mankind, have yet to be evangelised. We are ashamed that so many have been neglected. It is a standing rebuke to us and to the whole church. There is now, however, in many parts of the world an unprecedented receptivity to the Lord Jesus Christ. We are convinced that this is the time for churches and para church agencies to pray earnestly for the salvation of the unreached and to launch new efforts to achieve world evangelisation. A reduction of foreign

missionaries and money in an evangelised country may sometimes be necessary to facilitate the national church's growth in self-reliance and to release resources for unevangelised areas. Missionaries should flow ever more freely from and to all six continents in a spirit of humble service. The goal should be, by all available means and at the earliest possible time, that every person will have the opportunity to hear, understand, and receive the Good News. We cannot hope to attain this goal without sacrifice. All of us are shocked by the poverty of millions and disturbed by the injustices that cause it. Those of us who live in affluent circumstances accept our duty to develop a simple life-style in order to contribute more generously to both relief and evangelism. (John 9 v 4, Matt. 9 vs 35-38, Rom. 9 vs 1-3, 1 Cor. 9 vs 19-23, Mark 16 v 15, Isa. 58 vs 6-7, Jas. 1 v 27, 2 vs 1-9, Matt. 25 vs 31-46, Acts 2 vs 44-45, 4 vs 34-35).

Evangelism and Culture
The development of strategies for world evangelisation calls for imaginative pioneering methods. Under God the result will be the rise of churches deeply rooted in Christ and closely related to their culture. Culture must always be tested and judged by Scripture. Because man is God's creature, some of his culture is rich in beauty and goodness. Because he has fallen, all of it is tainted with sin and some of it is demonic. The Gospel does not presuppose the superiority of any culture to another, but evaluates all cultures according to its own criteria of truth and righteousness and insists on moral absolutes in every culture. Missions have all too frequently exported with the Gospel an alien culture, and churches have sometimes been in bondage to culture rather than to the Scripture. Christ's evangelists must humbly seek to empty themselves of all but their personal authenticity in order to become the servants of others, and churches must seek to transform and enrich culture, all for the glory of God. (Mark 7 vs 8,9 & 13, Gen. 4 vs 21-22, 1 Cor. 9 vs 19-23, Phil. 2 vs 5-7, 2 Cor. 4 v 5).

Education and Leadership
We confess that we have sometimes pursued church growth at the expense of church depth and divorced evangelism from Christian nurture. We also acknowledge that some of our missions have been

too slow to equip and encourage national leaders to assume their rightful responsibilities. Yet we are committed to indigenous principles and long that every church will have national leaders who manifest a Christian style of leadership in terms not of dominion but of service. We recognise that there is a great need to improve theological education, especially for church leaders. In every nation and culture there should be an effective training programme for pastors and laymen in doctrine, discipleship, evangelism, nurture and service. Such training programmes should not rely on any stereotyped methodology but should be developed by creative local initiatives according to Biblical standards. (Col. 1 vs 27-28, Acts 14 v 23, Tit. 1 vs 5 & 9, Mark 10 vs 42-45, Eph. 4 vs 11 & 12).

Spiritual Conflict
We believe that we are engaged in constant spiritual warfare with the principalities and powers of evil, who are seeking to overthrow the church and frustrate its task of world evangelisation. We know our need to equip ourselves with God's armour and to fight this battle with the spiritual weapons of truth and prayer. For we detect the activity of our enemy, not only in false ideologies outside the church, but also inside it in false gospels that twist Scripture and put man in the place of God. We need both watchfulness and discernment to safeguard the Biblical Gospel. We acknowledge that we ourselves are not immune to worldliness of thought and action, that is, to a surrender to secularism. For example, although careful studies of church growth, both numerical and spiritual, are right and valuable, we have sometimes neglected them. At other times, desirous to insure a response to the Gospel, we have compromised our message, manipulated our hearers through pressure techniques, and become unduly preoccupied with statistics or even dishonest in our use of them. All this is worldly. The church must be in the world; the world must not be in the church. (Eph. 6 v 12, 2 Cor. 4 vs 3-4, Eph. 6 v 11 & 13-18, 2 Cor. 10 vs 3-5, 1 John 2 vs 18-26, 4 vs 1-3, Gal. 1 vs 6-9, 2 Cor. 2 v 17, 4 v 2, John 17 v 15).

Freedom and Persecution
It is the God-appointed duty of every government to secure conditions of peace, justice and liberty in which the church may obey

God, serve the Lord Jesus Christ and preach the Gospel without interference. We therefore pray for the leaders of the nations and call upon them to guarantee freedom of thought and conscience, and freedom to practice and propagate religion in accordance with the will of God and as set forth in The Universal Declaration of Human Rights. We also express our deep concern for all who have been unjustly imprisoned and especially for our brethren who are suffering for their testimony to the Lord Jesus. We promise to pray and work for their freedom. At the same time we refuse to be intimidated by their fate. God helping us, we too will seek to stand against injustice and to remain faithful to the Gospel, whatever the cost. We do not forget the warnings of Jesus that persecution is inevitable. (1 Tim. 1 vs 1-4, Acts 4 v 19, 5 v 29, Col. 3 v 24, Heb. 13 vs 1-3, Luke 4 v 18, Gal. 5 v 11, 6 v 12, Matt. 5 vs 10-12, John 15 vs 18-21).

The Power of the Holy Spirit
We believe in the power of the Holy Spirit. The Father sent his Spirit to bear witness to his Son, without his witness ours is futile. Conviction of sin, faith in Christ, new birth and Christian growth are all his work. Further, the Holy Spirit is a missionary spirit; thus evangelism should arise spontaneously from a Spirit-filled church. A church that is not a missionary church is contradicting itself and quenching the Spirit. Worldwide evangelisation will become a realistic possibility only when the Spirit renews the church in truth and wisdom, faith, holiness, love and power. We therefore, call upon all Christians to pray for such a visitation of the sovereign Spirit of God that all his fruit may appear in all his people and that all his gifts may enrich the body of Christ. Only then will the whole church become a fit instrument in his hand that the whole earth may hear his voice. (1 Cor. 2 v 4, John 15 vs 26-27, 16 vs 8-11, 1 Cor. 13 v 3, John 3 vs 6-9, John 7 vs 37-39, 1 Thess. 5 v 19, Acts 1 v 8, Psa. 85 vs 4-7, 67 vs 1-3, Gal. 5 vs 22-23, 1 Cor. 12 vs 4-31, Rom. 12 vs 3-8).

The Return of Christ
We believe that Jesus Christ will return personally and visibly in power and glory to consummate his salvation and his judgment. This promise of his coming is a further spur to our evangelism for we remember his words that the Gospel must first be preached to all

Appendix 2 167

nations. We believe that the interim period between Christ's ascension and return is to be filled with the mission of the people of God who have no liberty to stop before the end. We also remember his warning that false Christs and false prophets will arise as precursors of the final Antichrist. We therefore, reject as a proud self-confident dream the notion that man can ever build a utopia on earth. Our Christian confidence is that God will perfect his kingdom and we look forward with eager anticipation to that day and to the new heaven and earth in which righteousness will dwell and God will reign forever. Meanwhile, we rededicate ourselves to the service of Christ and of men in joyful submission to his authority over the whole of our lives. (Mark 14 v 62, Heb. 9 v 28, Mark 13 v 10, Acts 1 vs 8-11, Matt. 28 v 20, Mark 13 vs 21-23, John 2 v 18, 4 vs 1-3, Luke 12 v 32, Rev. 21 vs 1-5, 2 Pet. 3 v 13, Matt. 28 v 18).

Conclusion

Therefore, in the light of this our faith and our resolve, we enter into a solemn covenant with God and with each other, to pray, to plan and to work together for the evangelisation of the whole world. We call upon others to join us. May God help us by his grace and for his glory to be faithful to this our covenant! Amen. Alleluia!

Notes

Notes

Notes

Notes

Notes

Notes

Notes

Notes

Notes